THE PAN BOOK OF
ETIQUETTE & GOOD MANNERS

ETIQUETTE and good manners are not just a stuffy set of rules. As a whole they are the graceful, the civilized and considerate way to behave. A knowledge of both is also of real practical value. It can help you to get and keep a job, to mix confidently and at ease with all kinds of people, to be poised at the grandest party and in the humblest home. It can open and smooth the way to a richer—in terms of cash as well as of friendship and experience—and more interesting life.

THE WAY you hold a knife and fork is etiquette; not making a guest feel awkward if he used the wrong knife and fork is good manners. Where the two conflict, good manners should always come first.

D1188754

THE PAN BOOK OF
ETIQUETTE AND
GOOD MANNERS

SARAH MACLEAN

A NEW BOOK EXPRESSLY WRITTEN FOR
PAN BOOKS LTD : LONDON

First published 1962 by
PAN BOOKS LTD.,
8 Headfort Place, London, S.W.1

Printed in Great Britain by Richard Clay and Company, Ltd.,
Bungay, Suffolk

CONTENTS

ACKNOWLEDGEMENT

I should like to thank the very many people who have so kindly gone out of their way to help me garner the facts in this book.

S. M.

CHAPTER 1

GETTING MARRIED

'ALL THE WORLD loves a lover' an etiquette book of the 1920s advised the engaged couple, 'but this does not keep the world from watching closely and criticizing severely any breach of good manners—especially on the part of the engaged girl.' The modern world is not so censorious—'society' no longer waits, one eyebrow at the ready, to be shocked. Today's engaged couple walk arm in arm in the street if they wish, go off for weekends alone together if they like and generally behave in a way that would have shocked their great grandmothers. The etiquette the modern engaged couple and their parents observe has nothing to do with shocking or not shocking—it is simply the best way to avoid hurting Aunt Emma's feelings and make relations between the two families as smooth and friendly as possible from the beginning.

THE ENGAGEMENT

Lady Cynthia Asquith, who married in 1911, writes that she and her mother sat cowering upstairs while her fiancé asked her father formally for her hand in the library. These days the young couple simply announce, 'We're engaged', and that's that. Parents who disapprove of their daughter's choice lie bravely that they're delighted, and hope for the best.

Since young people today have plenty of opportunity to get to know each other before deciding to get married most engagements are short, lasting only as long as is necessary to find somewhere to live and make the preparations for the wedding. For a Saturday afternoon spring wedding in a fashionable London church you may have to book as much as six months ahead.

Couples who are going to get married in a register office often consider it pointless to get engaged at all.

The boy's mother as soon as she hears the news should get

in touch with the girl's mother, say how pleased she is and arrange to meet if they haven't already done so.

When an announcement is to be put in the newspapers, it's important that close friends and relations should be told before it appears, as announcements are for acquaintances only.

Congratulations

Relations and friends who can't wish them well in person are supposed to write or send a telegram to either boy or girl, whichever they know. Tradition turns a blind eye on the fact that, as a marriage guidance counsellor says, in 80 per cent of cases it is the girl who brings the man to the point. The convention is to congratulate the man, never the girl. 'I'm so glad, I do so like John,' is roughly what most people say to the girl.

The Engagement Ring

Though it's more romantic for the young man to spring the ring as a surprise on his girl friend, most couples prefer to be practical and choose it together, as a ring that suits one hand may not suit another.

At one time it was invariably a precious stone—diamond, ruby, emerald or sapphire, and a young man coy about his finances arranged with the jeweller beforehand to show only those rings within his price range. These days many young couples discuss frankly how much he can afford, and often it is she who decides in favour of a secondhand ring free of purchase tax or a large and colourful semi-precious stone rather than an insignificant diamond, or spending money badly needed for their future home. Money apart, many girls prefer to be original rather than conventional—a case in point is the actress Heather Sears' engagement ring of garnet and seed pearls, bought off a barrow for five shillings.

But even the most modern and independent young woman still expects him to write the cheque.

Newspaper Announcements

Few people bother to announce their engagement in the newspapers unless they have a large social acquaintance, when

8

they put an advertisement in the Forthcoming Marriages section of *The Times* or *Telegraph, eg:*

MR F. L. NORTH AND MISS M. A. HAWKINS

The engagement is announced between Frederick Leonard, second son of Major and Mrs R. L. North of Well Lodge, Inkpen, Sussex, and Mary Anne, eldest daughter of Sir John and Lady Hawkins of 13 Wildcroft Street, London SW3.

A Broken Engagement

If the engagement has been announced in the papers another announcement should be inserted, like this:

The marriage arranged between Mr Alan Brown and Miss Jennifer Brooks will not take place.

When invitations have already been sent out each guest must be written to and told that the wedding is off. This unpleasant job usually falls to the bride's mother who simply states the fact briefly without going into who broke with whom or why.

If any presents have arrived the girl or her ex-fiancé, depending on whom they have been sent to, returns them to the giver with a note of thanks.

The girl is also supposed to return the engagement ring and any other valuable presents she may have received from her ex-fiancé. Obviously there is no point in returning anything he can't sell or give to anyone else.

The Wedding Ring

The couple choose it together and the bridegroom pays for it.

THE FORMAL WHITE WEDDING

This bristles with more problems and more points of etiquette than any other occasion a woman is likely to meet in her life unless she marries an ambassador or moves in royal circles.

As soon as they have agreed to get married, bride and groom should get in touch with the vicar of the church they have chosen, to settle the date and time of the wedding, the reading of the banns and the music at the ceremony.

If they are specially interested in the music, the vicar will arrange for them to meet the organist. The vicar or his vestry clerk may also arrange for flowers in the church—when two weddings take place on the same day, flowers are often shared—and printing of service leaflets.

Just before the wedding, most vicars will go through the prayers and responses with bride and groom and, if they like, supervise a rehearsal in the church.

Brides who prefer to promise to 'love and honour' only—not 'obey' their husbands—can, if the minister agrees, use the shortened marriage service in the 1928 prayer book, which leaves out the offending word.

At a fashionable London church all the fees are usually included in a bill sent out before the wedding. But the vicar will advise on what the fees are and when they should be paid. If a verger's fee is not included, he should be tipped from 10s to £1 on the day.

Who Pays?

Traditionally most of the onus of paying falls on the bride's parents. Here is the formula.

The bride's parents pay for: engagement and wedding announcements in the Press; wedding invitations; bride's dress and trousseau; wedding day photographs; printed leaflets for the service; decorations for the church; all hired transport for the bridal party on the wedding day except for the car hired by the groom for himself and his Best Man—the usual number of hired cars is four; all expenses to do with the reception.

The bridegroom pays for: the banns, or licence; marriage certificate; marriage service fee; verger's fee or tip; music in church; hired car for himself and Best Man; bouquets for bride and bridesmaids; buttonholes for bride's mother and his own mother; honeymoon.

The bridesmaids pay for their own dresses.

Obviously this formula can only be strictly observed where the bride's parents are comparatively well-off. Most people treat it as a basis and compromise according to their means. Very few brides these days can expect their parents to pay for an elaborate trousseau on top of all the other expenses and, when the bride is earning, the modern bridegroom usually expects her to pay her whack towards the honeymoon. Even when the bride's parents are well-off many bridegrooms offer to pay for all the hired transport and for the photographs.

Invitations

The bride and her mother send them out, having first asked the bridegroom's mother for her list of guests, telling her how many are planned for so that she knows how many she can fairly invite. When to send the invitations depends on how big the wedding is to be. The grander the affair, the earlier the invitations are sent out—but for a medium-sized wedding, four to five weeks is usual. A note from the bride's mother can be sent instead of a formal invitation, but this is plainly impracticable if there are more than a hundred guests.

Though the bridegroom's parents naturally expect to be at the wedding it is still customary to send them an invitation.

Presents

If you are asked for your wedding present list how business-like can you be without giving offence? Is it better to risk being called mercenary and list the exact make of china and colour of the bath towels you want or to risk winding up with a home cluttered with china in a design you can't stand and bath towels that clash with your walls? Most young couples with strong views on furnishings choose the former course, in the belief that their friends will prefer to give them something they really like. Lady Pamela Mountbatten and Mr David Hicks were examples of this modern tendency. They left an exact list of the presents they wanted in the shops where they were on sale. Several well-known London shops will keep these lists, crossing off each item as it is bought, which saves making and posting endless carbon copies. But there is one

11

tabu. Though you may prefer a cheque to a conventional present, it is still not tactful to ask unless you are offered the choice. Few people are generous enough to deny themselves the pleasure of giving something that will remind you of them when you use it.

There is no harm in asking for a grand piano if you want it and think there is a chance you may be given one, but it's only kind to your least well-off friends to include things in their price range too. Most people who receive an invitation to a wedding feel they ought to produce a present whether they accept or not.

The bridegroom is supposed to give the bridesmaids a present; this is generally a piece of jewellery, earrings, bracelet or brooch. Bride and groom are also supposed to give each other presents; the bride's present to the groom is often a watch or cufflinks, the groom's to the bride an eternity ring. Though modern bridegrooms are prone to a convenient lapse of memory over this convention!

Presents from the guests are sent before the wedding—either addressed in her maiden name, to the bride's home, or to the groom's if the giver doesn't know the bride—with a brief message on the enclosed card, such as: 'With love and best wishes for a very happy marriage, from Mary Brown.' It is charitable to send the present as early as possible so that the bride and groom can get their thank-you letters off before departing for their honeymoon. The fairest way is for the bride to thank for those presents that have been sent by her friends and relations, the groom for those that have been sent by his; though needless to say there are some husbands who make her write the lot.

Displaying Presents

They are rarely displayed except when the reception is held in a private house. If you are displaying them, what should you do about cheques? The usual procedure is to list 'Cheques From The Following:' and write the names of the givers but not the amounts. Other presents are displayed with their cards attached. If you have been given five toastracks, the

12

tactful thing to do is to space them out rather than bunching them all together.

Who Chooses Whom?

The groom chooses the Best Man and the ushers; the bride chooses the bridesmaids. The Best Man is usually the groom's best friend, the Chief Bridesmaid the bride's.

What the Best Man Does

The bridegroom is generally supposed to be in a high state of nerves on the day, and it's the Best Man's job to help him through his ordeal and see that he doesn't make any mistakes, that he's on time for the wedding and that he catches his train or plane for the honeymoon without leaving the luggage behind. The Best Man collects the bridegroom from his home and drives with him to the church; he takes charge of the wedding ring and makes any on-the-spot payments to the vicar or verger, or any last minute arrangements for the honeymoon the bridegroom may ask him to. The bridegroom should give him a sum of money to cover all expenses.

What the Chief Bridesmaid Does

She looks after the bride, making any last minute adjustments to the bride's dress in the church porch, supervising the other bridesmaids and usually helping the bride to change into her going-away clothes after the reception.

Arriving at the Church

Most fashionable weddings take place in the early afternoon.

The ushers should arrive half an hour, the guests about quarter of an hour before the time stated on the invitation card. The bride's mother and the groom's parents usually arrive just a few moments before the ceremony.

It is the ushers' job to ask guests: 'Friend of bride or groom?' and seat them accordingly, bride's friends and relations on the left of the aisle, groom's on the right. The left top pew is reserved for the bride's immediate family, the right top pew for the groom's. Other relations and VIPs should also be given a seat near the front.

13

Bridegroom and Best Man should arrive at the church about twenty minutes before the ceremony and go to the vestry to fix up any last minute formalities. They then wait for the bride either in the right hand pew or on two chairs in front. The bridesmaids arrive just before the wedding and wait for the bride in the porch.

The bride and her father arrive on the dot.

The Ceremony

The bride walks slowly up the aisle on her father's right arm, followed by the bridesmaids. Brides who are nervous of walking up a long, empty aisle may be preceded by the choir. The bride joins the bridegroom—bridegroom and Best Man stand up when the bride appears in the porch—in front of the chancel steps and stands on his left. Her father stands behind and to the left of her. The Best Man stands behind and to the right of the bridegroom. The Chief Bridesmaid comes forward and takes the bride's bouquet, and gloves if she's wearing them, then goes back to her place. Where the bridesmaids are adults, the Chief Bridesmaid is one of those in front; where the bridesmaids include children and adults or very young and older children, the smallest ones lead, but one of the adults or older children normally acts as Chief Bridesmaid. At Princess Margaret's wedding, where there were six child bridesmaids, it was Princess Anne from the back of the procession who came forward and took the bouquet.

When the minister asks: 'Who giveth this woman to be married to this man?' the bride's father, without speaking, steps forward, takes the bride's right hand and gives it to the minister, who puts it in the right hand of the bridegroom. After the plighting of the troth, the Best Man steps forward and gives the ring either to the clergyman or to the bridegroom, the clergyman will indicate which. The bridegroom then takes the ring and puts it on the bride's finger. The bride's father and the Best Man, when they have done their bit, usually remain standing, but they can if they like go and sit down.

After the ceremony is over, the minister leads the bridal couple into the vestry to sign the register, followed by both

14

sets of parents, the bridesmaids and the Best Man and, if the vestry is large enough, sometimes an old family friend. The bride signs her maiden name for the last time. The two witnesses are usually one from the bride's and one from the groom's side.

The bride then walks down the aisle on the groom's left arm, followed by the bridesmaids in pairs. If the bridesmaids are odd numbers, the Best Man may join the procession, otherwise he usually walks round the side of the church and waits in the porch. After the bridesmaids come the bride's mother with the groom's father, the groom's mother with the bride's father. Everyone then joins in behind, the top pews generally emptying first.

After the photographs have been taken outside the church, people leave for the reception, the bridal party in the hired cars first, in this order: bride and groom, bride's parents, bridegroom's parents, bridesmaids. Though at very lavish weddings a few hired cars are sometimes laid on for the guests, they are more often left to follow on as best they can in their own cars or in taxis. The Best Man and the ushers should stay behind to see that no one gets stranded.

The Reception

This is usually held a few minutes' drive from the church, in the bride's parents' house, a marquee on the lawn, a borrowed house, reception rooms or a hotel, and lasts on an average from two to two and a half hours. Grand cocktail party type food—canapés, vol au vents, sandwiches, etc—is laid out on a long buffet table. At a small wedding guests may be left to help themselves but, if the room is very crowded, it's obviously better, though more expensive, to have the food handed round. The traditional drink at a wedding reception is champagne, but some people economize by drinking a sparkling white wine and serving champagne only for the toasts. A peculiarity of the wedding reception is that no one is expected to do much in the way of introducing. The Best Man or an usher may rescue someone standing all alone, otherwise guests are left to introduce themselves.

Least expensive way to hold a reception is to have it at home, do most of the catering yourself with some help from the local bakery, buy your drinks from the local off-licence and hire someone on the day to help with cutting up the cake, handing round drinks and washing up. This, of course, is only possible with a small wedding. Alternatively you can get in a firm of caterers who will make all the arrangements, providing food, cake, drink, flowers, extra china, linen and waiters. Or you may arrange with them to provide your own cake and drink. There are firms of caterers who will go anywhere in the country. One firm of caterers will even arrange hired cars. If you hold the reception in a hotel, the hotel will also see to everything for you. The tip in a hotel is often paid at the same time as the bill and is usually five to ten per cent of the total. If you are hiring a firm of caterers ask the man you make arrangements with whom you should tip and how much.

The Receiving Line

Bride's mother, bride's father, groom's mother, groom's father, bride and bridegroom line up in that order inside the door of the reception room to receive guests. At a large wedding where there is a danger of the doorway becoming a bottleneck, the guests move quickly along the line, greeting and shaking hands with the parents, kissing the bride and telling her she looks lovely, if they know her well enough, and congratulating the bridegroom. At a small wedding, where there is no one to announce names at the door, it's a good idea to introduce yourself to anyone in the receiving line you don't know: 'I'm Mary Smith. I work in the same office as Belinda.'

The Cake

For a big wedding this is usually three tiers—the top tier is traditionally supposed to be kept for the christening party of the first child. Bride and groom cut the cake about twenty minutes after all the guests have been received—or appear to cut it. A wedding cake, sticky with fruit and brittle with icing can be tricky to carve and it is usually cut beforehand to save

the bride and groom wrestling with it. The waiters then take
the cake away to divide it into slices which are handed round
just before the toasts.

Toasts and Speeches

How many toasts and speeches you have is up to you. The
usual number is three. An old friend of the bride's family or
the bride's father says a few words about the bride, usually
some embarrassing anecdote about her childhood, wishes the
young couple happiness and finishes by proposing the toast to
the bride and groom. The bridegroom replies thanking the
bride's parents for the reception and the guests for their
presents and proposes a toast to the bridesmaids. The Best
Man replies, saying something complimentary about the
bridesmaids and a few words about the bridegroom. But at
fashionable weddings there is a growing tendency to have the
first two toasts only and cut out the Best Man's speech. At
the Duke and Duchess of Kent's wedding there were no
speeches at all, just a simple toast to the bride and groom.

At a large wedding there may be a special toast master to
announce the toasts. At a small wedding this isn't necessary;
the Best Man can simply ask for silence. The important thing
to remember if you are asked to make a speech is to keep it
light, since the tears of the bride's mother may be very near
the surface.

Here are some sample speeches:

Old Friend of Bride's Family

It is my pleasant duty to propose the toast to the bride and
groom. I have known Jane ever since I was asked to be her
godfather eighteen years ago. I little thought as she screamed
heartily at the font that she would turn into the serene beauty
she is today. I have known David for a very short time in
comparison—a mere two years—but what I have seen of him
reassures me that he will make my delightful god-daughter a
wonderful husband. Ladies and gentlemen, David and Jane—
here he holds up his glass—may they have every happiness and
success.

17

Bridegroom's Reply

This is supposed to be the bride's day, but I can assure you it is the most important day in my life, too. Thank you all for your good wishes and for so many lovely presents. I should also like to thank my parents-in-law for this wonderful party. Last but not least I should like to thank the bridesmaids for performing their task with such grace and charm. Ladies and gentlemen, I give you the toast to the bridesmaids.

Best Man's Reply

I know none of you want to listen to a long and tedious series of anecdotes from the Best Man. So I will simply say on behalf of the bridesmaids, thank you very much for the nice things you have said about them which I for one heartily agree with.

Telegrams

People who have received invitations to the wedding and can't come usually send a telegram, such as, 'Love and best wishes for a happy marriage.' The telegrams are often read out by the Best Man after the speeches. Some Best Men read them out before giving their speech to give themselves courage.

Going Away

Some time after the speeches, bride and groom go to change, the groom often accompanied by the Best Man and a bottle of champagne, the bride by the Chief Bridesmaid. Hotels and reception rooms provide special accommodation for this. The bridal couple go back into the reception room briefly before leaving, or someone may pass the rumour round or announce that they're ready to go. Everyone then crowds round the door to speed them on their way.

Guests are expected to leave shortly after the bride and groom, not before. If the bride's parents post themselves in the doorway, guests say goodbye and thank you, otherwise they simply drift off.

The old fashioned etiquette of writing a thank-you note to the bride's mother is seldom observed by young people today;

though any bride's mother after going to all the trouble and expense that arranging a wedding and reception entails may be glad to know that her guests enjoyed themselves.

The Wedding Breakfast

An alternative to the early afternoon wedding followed by a reception is a morning wedding followed by either a sit-down or a fork lunch, styled a wedding breakfast. Usual seating arrangements are: bride and groom at the head of the table, bridegroom on the bride's right. On the bridegroom's right, the bride's mother and next to her, the groom's father. On the bride's left sits her father and next to him the groom's mother.

FORMAL WHITE WEDDING CLOTHES

The Bride

The classic, full length, pure white dress with long tight sleeves and a train, like Princess Margaret's, is still the prettiest style and the one most often worn for large, fashionable weddings. It is also less likely to date than a short wedding dress—a point to remember when your wedding photograph is probably going to be with you for the rest of your life. Gloves are worn with short sleeves only, never with long sleeves.

The theme for brides is demure prettiness rather than sophisticated glamour—pale lipstick and not too much eye shadow. Jewellery should be kept to a minimum—pearls or diamonds for those lucky enough to have them. The engagement ring is worn on the right hand during the ceremony.

A white bouquet is the most appropriate, but it can be any colour. More important is that its size and shape should flatter the wearer—small, plumpish girls should carry a small slim bouquet that flows down the dress.

Bridesmaids

The bride chooses any colour she likes for their dresses, but rarely all-white or they might detract from hers. Princess Margaret's bridesmaids wore white, but their lily of the valley posies were tied with blue ribbon and the dresses had blue

19

ribbon at the neck and waistline. Lady Pamela Mountbatten's bridesmaids wore white with rose pink sashes.

When the bridesmaids are paying for their own dresses, the bride usually agrees to something that can be converted into a party dress afterwards or dresses made of some pretty but inexpensive material.

Mothers of Bride and Groom

They wear afternoon dresses or suits conventionally in grey or pastel shades, not black, and a frivolous hat.

Groom, Best Man, Ushers, Bride's Father

If the bride is wearing a formal white dress, strictly speaking they should wear morning dress, see page 181, and a white flower in their buttonholes.

Women Guests

They wear afternoon dresses or suits, not too décolleté, and always gloves and hats.

Men Guests

If the groom, Best Man, the ushers and the bride's father are wearing morning dress, they should wear morning dress, too.

Going-away Clothes

Most brides change into a pale-coloured suit, small hat, gloves and high heels, most grooms into a lounge suit.

INFORMAL CHURCH WEDDING

Some people prefer to get married quietly without all the fuss and expense of a formal white wedding and entertain a few friends to lunch or to drinks afterwards. In this case bride and groom get married in the clothes they're going away in— the bride in a suit and a pretty hat, the man in a dark lounge suit. The bride's father still gives her away and there is a Best Man, but bridesmaids are out of place.

REGISTER OFFICE MARRIAGE

If two people get married in a register office, there is no

reason why they shouldn't have a formal reception afterwards if they wish. In this case they invite only their nearest and dearest to witness the marriage in the register office and ask everyone else just to the reception. As they have no Best Man or bridesmaids there will be at most two speeches, and bride and groom will get married in their going-away clothes.

DINNER DANCE RECEPTION

Dancing at a wedding, once considered very 'lower class', is coming back into vogue. The Marquess of Milford Haven hired a jazz band for his party at Claridges.

There is a growing fashion for getting married as late as the vicar will allow in the afternoon and, instead of the conventional reception, holding a buffet dinner dance, which winds up with guests seeing the happy couple off at London airport.

But people still wear the usual wedding clothes.

NEWSPAPER ANNOUNCEMENTS

A wedding announcement in a national newspaper is worded like this:

SMITH : BROWN.—August 6th, 1962, at St Blank's Church, Oxford, JOHN BERNARD SMITH, eldest son of Mr and Mrs J. R. SMITH of Oxford, to SUSAN MARGARET, younger daughter of Dr and Mrs R. B. BROWN of Elmpond Square, London SW10.

Or if the wedding was a quiet one in a register office:

SMITH : BROWN.—August 6th, 1962, quietly in London, JOHN BERNARD SMITH, eldest son of Mr and Mrs J. R. SMITH of Oxford, to SUSAN MARGARET, younger daughter of Dr and Mrs R. B. BROWN of Elmpond Square, London SW10.

Some local newspapers which go in for detailed reports of local weddings will give you a form to fill up to ensure that all the details are correct.

In Church (Church of England)

(1) *By Special Licence*—With this licence, granted by the Archbishop of Canterbury, you can get married at any time and in any place, but these licences are only issued in very exceptional circumstances. Applications for a Special Licence must be made to the Faculty Office, No 1, The Sanctuary, Westminster, SW1.

(2) *After Banns*—When your marriage is to take place after the publication of banns, the banns must be called (*a*) if you and your fiancée live in the same parish, in the parish church of that parish or (*b*), if you live in different parishes, in the parish church of both parishes. Except in very special circumstances, when banns of matrimony have been published, the marriage must take place in the church or one of the churches in which the banns have been published. The banns must be published on three successive Sundays before you can get married.

(3) *By Bishop's Licence*—One of you must have lived for fifteen days immediately prior to your application in the parish in the church of which your marriage is to take place (subject to the exception in (4) below). Marriage licences are obtainable from the Diocesan Registry or a Surrogate, and the usual fee for the licence is £2 15s. You can be married on the same day as you get this licence.

(4) *In a Church which is 'usual place of worship'—by Licence or Banns*—This is an exceptional provision for people who attend and are on the Electoral Roll of a church outside the parish in which they live, and wish to be married in that church. Banns are then called in the church where the ceremony is to take place as well as in your parish church (or churches).

You can also get married in church according to the rites of the Church of England if your clergyman agrees, with a superintendent registrar's certificate. Though this, in fact, is rarely done.

Banns and licences alike hold good for three months only,

and except in the case of a special licence, the marriage must be celebrated between 8 am and 6 pm.

With a professional choir the cost of a big society wedding in one of the fashionable London churches may be as much as £30, not including flowers and service leaflets. Fees vary from parish to parish. In parishes where the Church Commissioners' standard table of fees is in force, the basic fees for a church wedding are:

	£	s	d
Publication of Banns		7	0
Certificate of Banns		3	6
Marriage after Banns		15	0
Marriage after Licence	1	10	0
Marriage after Superintendent Registrar's certificate	1	10	0
Additional fee for Choral Service	1	11	0
Certificate of Marriage		3	9
Special Licence	25	0	0
Bishop's Licence	2	15	0

In a Register Office

A Superintendent Registrar's certificate is necessary if you wish to get married in a register office. It can be issued with or without a licence.

Without a licence: If you both live in the same registration district you give notice of marriage to the Superintendent Registrar of that district. If you live in different districts you must give notice to the Superintendent Registrar of each district. You must then wait twenty-one days before you can be issued with a certificate. You must have lived in the district for the seven days before you give notice.

With a licence: You need give only one notice whether you both live in the same or different districts. But one of you must have lived in the district for the fifteen days before you give notice. You must then wait one clear day—other than a Sunday, Christmas Day or Good Friday—before you can be issued with your certificate and licence. You can then get married any time within three months from the day on which your notice was entered in the notice book.

Whether you get married with or without a licence, the notice can be given by either of you. Fees are:

	s	d
For entering notice of marriage in the marriage notice book	1	6
For a certificate of marriage	1	6
For a licence for marriage	45	0
For a marriage by certificate (without licence) in the presence of a Registrar	7	6
For a marriage by certificate (with licence) in the presence of a Registrar	15	0

EXPENSES AT RECEPTION

These vary enormously according to the quality of food and drink—the cake alone can cost anything from £10 to £100—how many waiters you have and where you hold your reception. A fashionable London hotel charges approximately £1 17s 6d a head for 100 guests; £1 15s a head for 200 guests; £1 12s 6d a head for 300 guests; £1 7s 6d a head for 400 guests, inclusive of food, drink, cake, reception and changing rooms, linen, china, cutlery, waiters and flowers. The same hotel estimates the cost of a wedding breakfast at £2 10s to £3 a head. The head waiter at this hotel doesn't expect to be tipped on the spot. A tip of about ten per cent of the total is usually added on to the account.

Caterers' prices range from about £2 10s a head excluding flowers and cake, down to £1 10s a head, for which one firm claims it can provide everything for the reception, including announcer of toasts and transport to and from the church. The £1 10s does not, of course, include the best champagne.

CHAPTER 2

OTHER MILESTONES IN A WOMAN'S LIFE

EXPECTING

Gone are the days when you only whispered the news to your mother and your closest friends and, as soon as ever it began to show, stuck close to your own hearthside knitting tiny garments and dreaming of the patter of little feet. Modern women often blazon the news abroad as soon as they know themselves—those who keep it a secret do so not from modesty but from fear that busy relations may be constantly on the phone asking for progress reports. They visit friends and go to parties right up until the last moment if they feel like it, and career women often carry on with their jobs for as long as their employer will allow, feeling that it makes the waiting seem less long.

But women, however modern, still like to wear clothes that camouflage as much as possible—the best and most attractive clothes for this purpose being straight adjustable skirts or slacks made of a firm material, topped by a huge sweater.

WHEN IT ARRIVES

An announcement of the birth is sent to either a local or national newspaper along these lines: On February 15th, 1962, at St Blank's Hospital, London, to Shirley (nee Brooks) and John Hedges, a daughter (Mary Anne).

Close relations and intimate friends usually send flowers and/or telegrams of congratulation—post offices sell special baby greetings forms—though many new mothers in hospital would much rather have a long gossipy letter than the umpteenth sheaf of gladioli. Small posies incidentally are more welcome than grand bouquets in wards where space and vases are limited.

Quote from one young mother: 'Why do visitors always

bring soft toys and little knitted jackets? I'd have liked something for me! Orange juice and barley water for instance to help down the masses of water I was made to drink, also a small bottle of toilet water.'

The baby's birth must be registered by mother or father within forty-two days—it's no good sending Granny along instead.

THE CHRISTENING

There is no etiquette about when it should take place but usually it is within the first three months for the purely practical reason that an older child may prove a difficult armful. Most christenings take place in the early afternoon, but some churches have their own rules as to days and times and it's advisable to consult the minister well in advance.

Godparents

The prayer book says that a girl should have two godmothers and one godfather, a boy two godfathers and one godmother. But there is nothing to stop you following the royal family's example and giving your child more or fewer godparents of either sex. Prince Andrew had five, 3 men and 2 women; Princess Anne also had five, 3 women and 2 men; Prince Charles had eight, 4 men and 4 women. They are generally chosen from among relatives and close friends and should belong to the same religious denomination as the child's parents, if the baptism service is not to be a mockery. Although all that most godparents these days feel is expected of them is to send the child presents on its birthdays, and a prayer book or bible on its confirmation.

Anyone unable to get to the service can become a godparent by proxy.

The Service

This is all written in the prayer book and is very simple to follow. The minister indicates to the mother and godparents when they should gather round the font, and the godparents read the responses. Usually one of the godmothers stands on the minister's left and gives the child to him to baptize, so she must hold it during the prayer before the prayer book says: 'then the priest shall take the child.' A godmother, the mother or a nurse holds it during the rest of the service. When the minister demands the name of the child, the godmother on the minister's left answers, giving the child's christian names, or all the godparents may answer together.

Where several babies are christened at the same service, the service is the same except that the minister says 'children' instead of 'child'.

What happens if your baby is mixed up with the one before and gets christened Gertrude Pearl instead of your carefully chosen Caroline Anne? This did happen once in the case of twin girls in a pram which was pulled rather than pushed to the church door. But the minister simply switched the names round in the register, and no harm was done.

After the service the father goes to the vestry and enters the baby's name in the register. As there is no fee for a christening, he should put something in the church box.

The Christening Party

Occasionally when a family is particularly eminent—when the child, for instance, is heir to a title—a christening is made an excuse for a grand party, formal invitation cards are sent out and the men wear morning dress. But in general, christenings are very informal affairs to which only relations and a few old family friends are invited, by letter or telephone. A lunch or tea party follows, either sit-down or buffet according to the numbers and space.

It's usual to provide a christening cake—either the top layer of your wedding cake or a white-iced cake with or without the baby's name on it—and a bottle of champagne in which to drink the baby's health. Otherwise food and drink is on an everyday level. The obvious person to propose the toast is a godfather, but there are rarely any speeches.

Clothes at a Christening

The men wear lounge suits, the women afternoon dresses or suits, pretty hats and gloves. The baby wears the family christening robe, if yours is the sort of family that has one, otherwise its best white frock.

Presents

Godparents always, other guests at a christening usually, produce a present. The traditional present is either silver—a mug, porringer, spoon and pusher, napkin ring—or jewellery —a child's bracelet or coral necklace or, in the case of the very rich, two or three pearls which were added to every birthday till the necklace was complete. These days presents tend to be more practical: money to start a post office account, savings certificates, a toy or a baby garment. Where silver is given it is likely to be something the child will be able to use when it is grown up—a bowl, cream jug or teaspoons.

WEDDING ANNIVERSARIES

There is no reason why you shouldn't celebrate any anniversary you please, but those most often made an excuse for a party are the Silver (twenty-fifth) the Golden (fiftieth) and the Diamond (sixtieth). The farthest the 'upper classes' go is to put an advertisement in the paper, ring up a few relations, order some champagne and a cake with a discreet little plaque and hold an informal family party. But there are still a great many people who feel that twenty-five years or more of marriage is worth celebrating with a grand do, and never mind whether it's non-U or not.

Here then are the main features of the celebration:

As many as possible of the people who were at the original wedding are invited. Husband and wife cut the cake together; it has silver decorations for a Silver or Diamond Wedding, golden decorations for a Golden Wedding. The couple's health should be drunk, the toast being proposed by the eldest son or the Best Man, and the husband should reply. For a very large party formal invitations are sometimes sent—in silver for Silver and Diamond Weddings, in gold for Golden Weddings.

Guests bring a present in keeping with the celebration. For a Silver Wedding, you might, for instance, bring something tied with a silver ribbon.

TELEGRAMS FROM THE QUEEN

If you write to the Queen's assistant private secretary enclosing a copy of the marriage certificate, the Queen will send a telegram of congratulation for a diamond wedding anniversary or any wedding anniversary after the sixtieth, at intervals of five years. Thus if you get a telegram from the Queen on your Diamond Wedding, you can get another one on your 65th, 70th and 75th wedding anniversaries.

TWENTY-FIRST BIRTHDAY

When a formal twenty-first birthday dance is given, formal invitation cards are sent and a toast is usually proposed, in which case, the hero or heroine of the hour should reply. But formal coming-of-age dances are rare even among girls who have been debutantes. Most parents feel they've done their bit by paying for a coming-out dance. They are more likely to give a cocktail party for which they send out ordinary At Home cards, or to treat their offspring and a party of his or her friends to the theatre and dinner afterwards. But where, as so often today, twenty-one-year olds have more money to spend than their parents they throw the party themselves—anything from a sophisticated cocktail party to a dancing to records beer-and-cheese affair, according to what their friends enjoy.

WHEN A DEATH OCCURS

Little is left of the elaborate and gloomy etiquette that used to surround a death. The general feeling these days is that grief is a private thing, ostentatious public display better avoided. Except in remote parts of the country, blinds are no longer pulled down in the house and, instead of each member of the family in turn morbidly sitting up with the corpse all night, the dead usually remain at the undertaker's until the funeral.

Funerals tend to be simple and quiet. Long black processions following the hearse through the streets are rare. The custom is growing for the immediate family only to follow the coffin to the graveside, friends attending the service in church or chapel and leaving immediately afterwards.

Men wear morning suits only at the funerals of very eminent persons—the sort of funeral that takes place at Westminster Abbey, otherwise they wear dark lounge suits and a black tie.

Women wear black if they happen to have it, otherwise something plain and dark.

Arrangements

The doctor's certificate must be taken to the register office and the death registered before the arrangements for the funeral can be made; the death must be registered within five days. The clergyman if he's a friend can be called in to advise on an undertaker. Alternatively the undertakers—or funeral directors as they prefer to be called—can advise on a church service and get in touch with the clergyman for you. The undertakers will also, if you like, cope with newspaper announcements and, if many people are expected at a large country funeral, arrange for cars to meet the train.

Newspaper Announcements

Few people feel like writing to inform anyone except relations and intimate friends when a death occurs. Instead they put an announcement in the local or national newspapers including the time and place of the funeral service so that anyone who wants to may attend. Announcements are on these lines:

> On January 1st, 1961, at —— Hospital, John Smith, after a long illness. Service at St Luke's Church, London SW3, on January 8th at 11.30. Cremation at Golders Green, family only. Flowers to (address of undertakers).

Sometimes people request 'No flowers, please', and ask for donations to be sent instead to a charity the deceased was interested in.

Flowers

They should be sent to arrive on the morning of the funeral at the address given in the announcement, with the name of the sender and a brief message of sympathy on the attached card—'In loving memory', 'In deepest sympathy', or whatever your feelings dictate. The name of the deceased preceded by 'The late' is written on the envelope.

Letters

It is still etiquette to write a letter of sympathy as soon as you hear of the death. People who feel these letters only prolong the agony can include in the announcement of the death the request: 'No letters, please.'

The bereaved relative should write and thank everyone who has sent flowers and/or a letter of sympathy. A single sentence will do—simply, 'Thank you for your beautiful flowers and kind sympathy.' But sometimes when this would entail a large correspondence printed cards of thanks are sent instead to people who are not intimate friends and relations. Alternatively acknowledgements may be placed in the newspapers.

> The family of the late Mr David Smith wish to thank all relations and friends for kind expressions of sympathy and beautiful flowers received during their sad bereavement.

But sticklers for old-fashioned etiquette might consider this rather casual.

The Service

The service can either be held in church, the body being taken afterwards to crematorium or cemetery, or in the case of cremation the dead can be taken straight to the crematorium and the service held in the crematorium chapel. A few cemeteries also have chapels where a service can be held.

If the dead was not a practising Christian there is no need to have a religious service, although such a barren end is exceedingly rare.

After the Funeral

If there are only a few people at the funeral the custom is for the bereaved relative to invite them back to the house for a drink or a cup of tea to cheer them on their way home.

Mourning

Formerly there was an elaborate etiquette and a fixed time of mourning according to degrees of kinship: two years for a husband, one year and nine months' full mourning (mainly black), three months' half mourning (grey, lavender, purple or black and white), diamonds permissible before the end of the first year, gold ornaments not; one year for a parent, six months' full mourning, six months' half mourning, the wearing of diamonds, but not gold, permissible at the end of three months. . . . There were rules, too, about when it was correct to enter society again. Anyone who didn't abide by these rules risked social criticism.

These days mourning is purely a matter for the individual and how he or she feels. Few men wear black ties except at the funeral and fewer still wear black armbands. As for women, the blacks and lavenders once considered mourning colours are now fashion colours and no longer carry any special significance. Black borders are no longer used on cards and letters.

Most people prefer to keep their sorrow to themselves, picking up the threads of normal life as soon as they cheerfully can.

CHAPTER 3

THE HOUSEWIFE

THIS CHAPTER begins where every housewife's job begins—
with furnishing the new home. 'Common' or, more modernly,
'non-U', sound repulsively snobbish when applied to the way
a home is furnished, but almost invariably the objects that
prompt this description are, in fact, in bad taste. The mantel-
piece may be cluttered with ugly, sentimental and mass-
produced ornaments such as the all-too-familiar three ducks
in flight, china alsatian dogs and Negroes' plastic heads. There
may be gnomes in the garden. Cushions may be set on their
points, furniture and carpets placed diagonally to the wall,
tablecloths laid corner to corner, because their owners feel
there is something coarse about things that are set square—
this is what is meant by 'genteel'. Perhaps there are anti-
macassars on the chairs and duchesse sets fussing up the
dressing tables; or, worst of all, curtains hung facing the street
instead of, as they should be, to improve the appearance of the
room.

What is good taste in furnishing? Suitability of furniture to
the house—a grandiose piece of furniture is ridiculous in a
cottage—harmonious arrangement and good design. Good
design is a question of form, proportion, pattern and colour.
And everything in the house from the cutlery to the armchairs
can be well or badly designed. The only way to find out what
good design is, is to look at it, study the home magazines and
go to exhibitions of furniture and furnishings.

Though it's a great deal easier to make a home look attractive if you have a good deal of money it's still by no means
impossible without. A great deal of mass produced furniture
is ugly—but not all, as a visit to the Design Centre in the Hay-
market, London, to see the pick of British design will show.
Alternatively, an attractive antique can often be bought for

less than a hideous piece of so called 'modern' furniture made of inferior wood.

A play safe course is to paint your rooms all-white, stick to the bare minimum of furniture, Scandinavian or furniture shown in the Design Centre, use only plain-coloured or striped fabrics and go in for eye-level lighting and pictures, rush matting and pale, polished wood floors.

But to follow slavishly a particular fashion is a crying waste of an exciting opportunity to develop personal taste and talent and to be, in one's own way, an artist.

PICTURES AND ORNAMENTS

The mistake most often made is to buy them for their subject rather than for their own aesthetic value. An enchanting landscape painted by your aunt may not make nearly such a good picture as a gasworks painted by an artist. The safe pictures, of course, for those wary of their own taste, are any of the very excellent prints of famous paintings that can be bought comparatively cheaply.

GETTING TO KNOW THE NEIGHBOURS IN THE COUNTRY

For most of us today the best way to get to know our neighbours in the country is to join in communal activities such as the Women's Institute where women from all walks of life meet. The old-fashioned and complicated ritual of card-leaving is still practised only by a very few elderly 'county' types in a few remote parts of the country. Most people brought up in the days when everyone who was anyone left cards for every conceivable reason, packed their cards away and forgot about them during the second world war.

But if, after moving to a new district in the country, you should come home one day to find on your doormat three little white cards engraved with the name of a retired admiral and his wife, you should know what's going on. The largest of the cards would bear the name of the admiral's wife; the two smaller ones, the admiral's name, the etiquette behind this being that a man was supposed to call on both men and women, a woman on other women only.

The polite thing to do would be to return their call, that is,

34

just turn up on their doorstep one afternoon, and if they're not in, leave some record of your visit. Some women living in a district where this sort of 'calling' still goes on compromise with the old-fashioned etiquette and have large good quality white cards simply engraved with their name in copperplate lettering:

Mrs John Black

These they use with a scribbled message on the back simply to show they have been and found the owners of the house out. There is, however, absolutely no need to have any cards at all today, however 'county' you may be.

But for a young couple new to a country district it would still be tactful to let elderly residents make the first friendly approach.

COMPLAINTS

This is one of the many cases where good manners are good strategy. Supposing you live in a flat in town and the people next door keep you awake every night. You can thump on the wall and yell at them to be quiet, for goodness' sake! But nine times out of ten you will get far better results if you invite them in to coffee in a friendly way and in due course let it be known that your husband has insomnia and could they try to be a little quieter.

The same applies if you're in the wrong yourself. Your cat spends its spare time rooting up your neighbour's seeds and she sends you a peremptory little note. Go and see her, explain how difficult it is to keep the cat in, but you will do what you can. Probably you will be able to work something out together and good relations will be restored.

GIVING A PARTY

If it's likely to keep other people in the building awake, it's only considerate to forewarn them. There's all the difference in the world between being told two days in advance by the young couple upstairs that they're going to give a birthday party and they hope you'll look in for a drink, and simply waking up one night to find all hell let loose on your ceiling.

And from the hosts' point of view it's well worth a few drinks to keep on friendly terms with other residents and ensure against the party being brought to a wretched end by furious shouts and threats to complain to the landlord.

Borrowing

Few people mind lending the odd bit of tea, sugar or butter to the people in the next flat when they've run out. But they do mind if they are never paid back. Even if they're not hard up for money they may be hard up for shopping time. The only way to deal with the borrower who never pays anything back is never to have any tea, sugar or butter when she asks for it.

When money is borrowed it should always be returned as soon as ever possible.

Television Manners

Treating the television as a background for conversation is one of the grimmest of failures in the social graces today. Anyone unused to hearing it blaring away all the time finds it more than a little trying to have to compete. When visitors come the television should be turned off unless they have come expressly to see it or they are close friends who drop in without any warning, when it would be fair to say, 'Do you mind if we just watch the end of this?' then switch off when the programme comes to an end. Otherwise guests may be justified in presuming that their hosts find the television more entertaining than their company. Though this may well be true it's not tactful to let them know!

But the blank face of a television set has a mesmeric effect. Let it stare at you for long enough and it practically wills you to turn it on. That is why it has become the 'smart thing' to have the television in its own room or the bedroom—anywhere except the sitting room.

Manners for Modern Children

The infant prodigy who sits up to dinner and monopolizes the conversation, upsetting the digestion of all but its proud parents, is becoming an all too familiar figure on the social

36

scene. Often this little monster is the child of intelligent, charming and considerate parents who, because they are fearful of repressing the child's personality, allow it to do exactly what it likes, and never correct it. No one would want the return of the seen-and-not-heard days when the little boy watched his father eat the slug in the salad, too frightened to tell him. But there is a happy medium. A child can have good manners without being repressed. Indeed, these days, when families tend to live more and more in each other's pockets, it is essential a child should have good manners if we are not to repeat the pattern of American home life where Junior's whims rule the household.

Here then is my analysis of what the well-brought-up child today does and doesn't do.

He gets up when adult visitors come into the room and greets them politely. He calls them Mr, Mrs or Miss unless asked to call them by their christian names. When his mother takes him with her to a meal at a friend's house, he eats neatly, sits quietly while adults are talking, says his piece now and then and, when it is time to leave, says 'goodbye' and 'thank you'.

When people are standing in buses and trains he offers to give up his seat; if he is too young to stand, his mother should take him on her knee.

He doesn't treat his parents' friends as an audience to show off to. He doesn't monopolize the conversation, nor does he interrupt when other people are speaking. He doesn't keep asking for things. He doesn't howl with wrath when visitors come and the children's television is switched off. He doesn't stand on the furniture. He doesn't answer back. He doesn't mimic adults, in front of them at any rate. Needless to say, he doesn't suck iced lollies all over a train compartment.

MONEY PRESENTS

Traditionally, the well-brought-up child doesn't accept them except from relations. But times are changing. As one little girl from a very respectable home said the other day when asked if her mother would allow her to accept a tip: 'Oh, Mummy's only too glad when we're given money!'

SCHOOLS

Parents wishing to send their children to a private or public school should make sure there is a vacancy well before the child is ready to go. Not only boys these days, but girls also are put down at birth for some of the more popular schools. People who have the money to send their children to this kind of school often put them down for several and make the final choice later on.

But even at small private schools there is often a long waiting list and if you wait to see whether your child fails the eleven-plus it may be too late to find her a place in the school of your choice. Write to a London scholastic agency, stating your price range and any other special requirements, such as the district you'd like the school to be in, and you will be sent free of charge the prospectuses of suitable schools that have vacancies.

If you want to see the headmaster or headmistress, ring up the secretary and ask for an appointment. Headmasters and headmistresses rarely need to see the child as well. A recommendation from another parent whose child has been to the school can help a great deal when there's a waiting list.

If there is a uniform, no matter how hideous, it is kind to let your child have it. A child, especially a new boy or girl, given a special dispensation to wear a brown coat when the others are all wearing green ones, can be made to feel a freak by staff as well as other children. It's etiquette at school for children to look as much alike as possible!

Where parents can't afford the uniform at a grammar school the local education authority in most districts is empowered to make a grant.

THE DOCTOR

What do you do if you want a second opinion? The easiest as well as the most courteous way is first to ask your doctor. Though doctors are not obliged to call in a second opinion if they don't consider it necessary, usually they are quite willing to.

If you want to change your doctor, you can simply go to

38

a new doctor and leave it to him to make the arrangements with your old doctor. But the polite thing to do is to let your doctor know yourself. If you are moving to a new district you can get the names of the local doctors from the local authority —a list of doctors is also to be found in most main post offices. In an emergency, if you can't contact your own doctor, you can go to any National Health doctor and get free treatment.

Supposing your doctor has been specially kind to you or your family, can you without embarrassing him give him a present? Doctors do in fact get quite a number of presents, especially at Christmas time, usually impersonal things such as a bottle of wine or whisky, cigarettes or cigars.

DENTISTS

They often complain that patients don't let them know when they can't turn up for an appointment. This is another instance of good manners paying off. If you let your dentist know, he's less likely to charge you for a missed appointment. If you let him know in good time, of course, he wouldn't dream of charging you.

IN HOSPITAL

Maddening as it is to watch your nurse after she's removed the thermometer purse her lips and hide your own temperature from you, dismissing your questions with a smilingly vague: 'Nothing to worry about,' this is hospital etiquette. The nurses are not supposed to tell patients what's the matter with them. It's up to the doctor to tell you or not, according to whether he feels it would be good for you to know.

Supposing you can never keep him long enough by your bedside to question him? Then your best course is to ask the ward sister. She may tell you herself, especially if she thinks you're worrying about having some dread disease which you haven't in fact got. If she feels it's not her business to tell you, you can ask her to let the doctor know that you'd like to see him.

Alternatively your next of kin can always ask to see the doctor or specialist in charge of your case.

The person to get hold of on the telephone if you want to visit a patient out of normal visiting hours or to find out how he is, is the ward sister. But only the next of kin or the person standing in for next of kin will be told the details. Anyone else will have to be satisfied with such stock generalizations as: Fairly comfortable, passed a good night. This again is hospital etiquette.

Presents

Though there is no need for a patient to give anything to anyone when she leaves hospital or nursing home, if a nurse has been specially kind many people give a box of chocolates, a pair of nylons, a book token or a couple of theatre tickets. Alternatively, one might give a large box of chocolates for all the nurses in a ward. But there are hospitals where nurses are not allowed to accept presents, there are also some nurses who are embarrassed by them. In this case, the best thing to do is to give something towards the hospital fund that provides extra comforts for nurses.

Another good way to say thank you is to write to the hospital matron mentioning the nurse by name—this helps a student nurse with her reports. Even if she is no longer a student, it will still be welcome. Letters of appreciation from patients help to make nursing, which involves long hours for rather low pay, seem worthwhile.

Patients with private rooms sometimes tip the ward maids, but not all ward maids will accept tips.

SHOPPING

Household shopping can be one of the trials of the early days of marriage. You ask for a pound of steak and while you're wondering if you can fairly say, 'Not that piece', the butcher has cut you off a slab of something you don't like the look of at all. Too shy to protest, you meekly accept it and at dinner your husband complains it is tough. Shopkeepers expect you to insist on getting what you want, and if you don't, if you find you've been given a bad pineapple for instance, it's perfectly fair to take it back.

What should you do when you're trying on a garment and the assistant stands at your elbow continually telling you how nice it looks and leaving you no time to make up your own mind? The best shop assistants don't do this, knowing that if they force you to buy something you're not going to like, the chances are you won't come back to that shop again. But if you meet one who does, tell her firmly and politely that you'd like to be left alone and that you'll come out and tell her when you've made your decision.

It's all too easy to be bullied into buying something that doesn't suit you by remarks like: 'You'll never get anything that fits you better than that Madam', or: 'That's how they're being worn nowadays', when the thing is plainly two sizes too big.

But there is another side to the picture—the customer who treats an assistant like dirt knowing that she is in no position to answer back. It is not fair to try on everything in the shop and waste some poor assistant's time when you have no intention of buying. Many shop assistants depend for their living on the commissions they get on sales.

Complaints

The fair course when one has a complaint to make about a purchase is to seek out the assistant who sold it and complain to her. Only if she can't or won't put things right should one ask to see the manager.

How to open an Account

All you have to do is fill in a form and produce a bank reference and usually two business references as well. These could be two local shops that know that your credit is good.

How to open a Bank Account

Simply go into the bank you have chosen and tell one of the cashiers you wish to open an account. He will then probably arrange for you to see the manager, and you will be asked for the name and address of someone who can give you a reference. This should be someone who has a bank account —not necessarily at the bank you have chosen—and who has known you for some time.

Customers are entitled to see their bank manager at any convenient time and ask his advice on any matter on which he's competent to give it, what investments to sell out and whether such and such a house is worth buying, for instance. At a big city bank you may have to wait longer than you would at a small provincial branch, but your bank manager will never refuse to see you.

The time you must see your branch manager is when you are contemplating overdrawing your account. If you do this you are borrowing the bank's money and it's only courteous to let him know.

You will be shown how to make out a cheque when you open your account. But there is a point of etiquette here. Though from the bank's point of view it is quite correct to make a cheque out to M. L. Smith, it is more polite to make it out to Miss, Mr or Mrs M. L. Smith. Cheques should always be endorsed, when necessary, in the same way as they are made out. If a cheque is made out to you as Miss Mary Smith, you should sign it Mary Smith, not M. L. Smith.

Letters to the bank are addressed to the manager—in spite of the fact that he's very unlikely to read most of them—begin 'Dear Sir' and end 'Yours truly (or faithfully)'. But customers who have met him often, begin 'Dear Mr Smith' and end 'Yours sincerely'.

SUBSTITUTE FOR SERVANTS

'Lady Swordstick is pleased to say that the reference of Jane Duster is satisfactory and she would be glad therefore if she would enter her service as housemaid on June 10th, as was arranged.' This imperious little note was, according to an old-fashioned etiquette book, the correct way to engage your staff in 1927. Jane Duster started work at 6.45 in the morning, received a pound a week pay, got one afternoon off a week, and every other Sunday for church.

How times have changed is illustrated by an advertisement which appeared in the Domestic Situations Vacant column of a national newspaper: 'Cook-general, £10 a week, plain cooking for two adults, own comfortable flat with television, two days off a week.'

Old-fashioned servants have disappeared from all but the richest households. In their place are the 'helps' whose status is very different from poor little Jane Duster's. And the question these days is not seeing that they do their work satisfactorily so much as treating them well enough so that they stay with you and don't seek more congenial employment elsewhere.

The Daily Help

She is paid by the hour anything from 2s 6d to 5s depending on the district you live in and the amount of work she does for you. If she works every day for you, she is more likely to accept 2s 6d an hour than if she comes only twice weekly. If she doesn't live locally, her fare is usually paid as well.

Unless she is a young girl, it is usual these days to call her Mrs Blank and she will probably call you Mrs Blank, too.

The Living-in Help

These days she is usually a girl from abroad, obtained either through friends or an agency; a leading London agency has at most two or three English people applying for domestic jobs in a year. In order to get the necessary work permit from the Ministry of Labour you must fill in a form stating the hours of work and what you intend to pay her; the point of this being that she must not be paid less or made to work longer hours than an English girl doing the same job. Employment exchanges will advise on local rates.

Who pays the fare varies. Many employers advance the fare then deduct it from the girl's wages, but pay the money back to her if she stays for a year.

Time Off

The minimum is two half days or one full day a week and a fortnight's holiday with pay. Evenings off is a vexed question, but most employers would allow her to go out after dinner, if she asked permission, in the knowledge that if she isn't happy in her present job there are plenty of others going.

43

Laundry and Telephone

Most employers allow her to send her towels and sheets to the laundry if they use one, but expect her to do her personal washing herself. Local telephone calls are usually on the house, unless she has a great many. If she had frequent long trunk calls it would be fair to ask her either to pay for them herself or to cut them short in future.

Work

Obviously it is unfair to expect her to do all the housework, the cooking and look after the baby. One housewife allots the work like this: she does most of the cooking and looks after the baby; the help does the cleaning and the washing-up and prepares the vegetables. Any big job such as washing the curtains or cleaning out the cupboards is shared.

The foreign girl helps to bring the food into the dining room but does not do any formal waiting at table. She eats the same as her employers do except when they are giving a dinner party and there may not be enough to go round.

What to call Her

If she comes from abroad and has been in domestic service there she usually expects to be called by her christian name whatever her age. If she is English, the modern tendency is only to call her by her christian name if she is a young girl and for her to call you Mrs Blank rather than Madam.

Friends and 'Followers'

These days most employers would allow her to entertain her friends, including boy friends, in her own room or, if it's a large house, in the kitchen. In a flat, some people allow her to entertain her friends in the sitting room when they go out for the evening. However, before making a concession like this, it is obviously wise to wait and see what the girl and her friends are like.

The Au Pair Girl

Between fifteen and twenty, all she needs in order to get into the country is a letter from you inviting her to stay in your household under the au pair system. This means that she will expect to live as one of the family and help you with light household tasks, not working any harder than a member of the family would. In return, she will expect pocket money—this is usually about 30s, but it does vary between £1 and £2. If she's a student, and the system was originally designed for girls who wanted to learn English, she must be given time off for classes as well as recreation. She pays her own fare over but her hosts often offer to pay her fare money back if she stays more than six months.

Though some people find this system works well, it is open to abuse on both sides. Either the girl does no housework or she is made to do an unfair share. One Swedish girl who came over to this country at the age of eighteen found herself expected to look after two children, do all the cooking and the housework in a large Georgian house with four reception rooms. For this she received £2 a week!

But taking advantage of the au pair system in this way doesn't pay in the long run. The au pair girl can always move to someone else. When she lands in this country she is given a list of authorities she can go to for help if she's not happy.

Another reason why the au pair system often comes to grief is that a pretty young foreign girl constantly asking his advice on how to pronounce this and how to say that in English can prove far too attractive to a middle-aged husband.

The Baby-Sitter

At anything from 2s an hour for the teenage girl next door to 4s an hour as charged by some baby-sitters in London, a baby-sitter can make the most modest evening out an expensive luxury. A baby-sitter expects to do nothing but sit and see that the baby comes to no harm. If it is to be an all-evening session she will expect to be left something with which to cook herself a meal and, if her return home involves a long walk in the dark, your husband should offer to drive her back or pay for a taxi.

References

Many people will engage staff on trust these days and risk having the odd thing stolen rather than having to scrub the

45

floor themselves. Nine times out of ten nothing will be stolen. But there are some dishonest people in every walk of life and if you have anything valuable in the house it is obviously wise and reasonable to get a reference. Simply ask for the name and address of the last employer and ring her up or write to her. Always ask exactly what you want to know. An ex-employer may not volunteer the information that your prospective help isn't trustworthy unless you ask the question point blank, 'Is she honest?'

CHAPTER 4

THE CAREER WOMAN

THE FIRST essential for getting ahead in any career is efficiency but, since the success of a firm depends on team work rather than the ability of isolated individuals, an easy and pleasant manner and a capacity for fitting in run a very close second. A pattern that constantly recurs is that where two girls are equally competent one gets passed over and the other gets promotion, the reason being that one has a gauche manner and a prickly personality, the other gets on with people, is a pleasure to work with and a credit to the firm.

This is largely a question of courtesy and consideration for others. But the business world is different from the social world outside, it has its own quirks of etiquette and its own pitfalls. There are many situations in which knowing the form can help to smooth the newcomer's path. It can also help her to land the job in the beginning.

LETTER OF APPLICATION

Writing this letter is writing an advertisement for yourself and how you phrase it and set it out is immensely important—especially if there is a lot of competition for the job.

The golden rule is that it should be easy to read, neatly set out, clearly and precisely expressed and as brief as possible. The letter should be typed unless otherwise stated in the advertisement. Like all business letters, it should have the name and/or status of the person you are writing to and his address either on the top or the bottom left-hand side of the page. Your name should be typed under your signature with Miss or Mrs beside it.

A busy employer has neither the time nor the patience to wade through pages of irrelevant waffle, so go straight to the point. State (1) what job it is you are applying for: 'I am applying for the job of secretary advertised in the *Daily*

Blank, June 5th.' (2) What qualifications and experience make you suitable for the job (shorthand and typing speed in the case of a secretary, what jobs you have held and how long for, any relevant certificates or diplomas). (3) Why you want the job—this is your opportunity to show originality, personality and a keen interest in the work. Unless asked to state your terms in the advertisement it's not advisable at this stage to mention pay and hours. (4) Your age. (5) When you can come for an interview: 'I could come for an interview any afternoon next week', never, 'Should this application meet with your approval, I shall be glad to place myself at your disposal for an interview at your convenience.' Long-winded and obsequious cliché phrases of this kind will lose you a job for which there is any competition.

If all the information won't fit on one side of a sheet of writing paper, the best plan is to list qualifications and experience with dates on a separate sheet and write a brief covering letter.

'Yours sincerely', is the correct way to end, if you write to a prospective employer by name, 'Yours faithfully' if you begin 'Dear Sir (or Dear Madam)'. Never 'Yours hopefully', or 'Yours in anticipation'!

Gimmicks such as elephantine envelopes adressed in green ink may pay off if you're going into advertising or publicity, but my advice is to steer clear of them in any other business. An employer may think you don't know the correct way to address an envelope or that it should fit the writing paper inside.

THE INTERVIEW

The first essential is to get there on time. Arriving late is not only rude and inefficient, it will make you flustered, too. It's a wise precaution to allow a few minutes for getting lost in a maze of passages, being sent up to the office of the wrong Mr Adams or any of the host of accidents that have a way of happening if you arrive on the dot. Give your name to the receptionist: 'My name's Miss Smith. I have an appointment with Mr Adams', and offer to wait if you're early. You will have to wait a few minutes in any case while your interviewer is told you are there.

Anybody tempted to discuss Mr Adams with another occupant of the waiting room should bear in mind the following cautionary tale: One girl nervous about her approaching interview with the editor of a well-known magazine asked the pleasant-looking man sitting opposite her if the editor was as awful as gossip held him to be. Not until she had related the fruity worst did she discover she was, in fact, talking to the editor!

Probably a secretary will come and collect you, open the office door for you, announce you and close the door behind you. But your interviewer may collect you himself, in which case, if he's got any manners, he will stand aside to let you enter the office first. If your interviewer is a woman, it would be polite to let her go first.

Say good morning or good afternoon to your interviewer, but wait for him to offer to shake hands. The tactful course throughout the interview is to leave the initiative with him, stand until he asks you to sit, don't smoke unless he offers you a cigarette (don't, whatever you do, go into his office smoking —he may regard his office as his castle and take it as a personal insult), wait for him to ask the questions. There is only a limited number he can ask you and you should have been able to foresee them and know roughly what you are going to say beforehand. A question he will almost certainly ask is why you want to leave your present job, and in answering this it's not good policy to run down your employers. He may get the impression you're not likely to be happy anywhere. If you have been out of a job for some time, he will probably want to know the reason.

But there are bad interviewers. What should you do if he appears at a loss for what to ask? Prompt him with something of this kind: 'Would you like me to tell you exactly what work I did in my last job?'

Some interviewers pride themselves on tricky questions such as: 'Tell me about yourself, Miss Smith.' The answer to this one is to do just what he asks. Tell him what your parents did for a living, where you went to school, what your hobbies are, high-lighting anything particularly to your credit, that scholarship you won for instance.

Another tricky question is: 'What can I tell you about the job?' Don't be lulled into thinking this means the job's yours for the asking and your signature on the dotted line and start talking about pay and time off. Stick to asking about the work, using any cues that present themselves to show just why you are the right person for the job. Leave it to him to bring up the question of terms. An employer has to be very desperate to take on someone whose prime reasons for taking a job are the salary and holidays.

If you're unlucky enough to come across the interviewer who deliberately tries to embarrass you by beginning: 'What can I do for you, Miss Smith?' your only possible reply is to throw the ball right back to him: 'You asked me to come and see you about a job, Mr Adams.'

Your Manner at the Interview

This is one of the occasions in life when you have to forget everything anybody ever told you about modesty and blow your own trumpet. If you say that you don't think you can do the job your interviewer is not likely to think so either. The difficulty here is to give the impression of quiet confidence in your ability rather than cock-sureness, remembering that you are being interviewed not only to find out how able you are but also whether you're likely to get on with the rest of the staff. You will get good marks for pleasant, unaffected manners and a sense of humour, but it's unwise to show this at the expense of the firm's products, as one man discovered when being interviewed for a job in advertising. His crack about the immorality of the advertising game was met by a moment of poker-faced silence followed by a lecture to the effect that the country's economy depended on it.

Clothes for the Interview

Exactly what clothes you wear depends on the kind of job you are after. If it's anything to do with fashion obviously your clothes should be as up to date and chic as possible. You're unlikely to land the job if you turn up in a skirt two dowdy

50

inches longer than anybody else's. It's good policy too to choose your interview clothes with an eye to fashion if the job involves meeting people outside the firm and acting as its representative.

But most important, whatever the job, is to look well-groomed. Polished shoes, neat hair, clean gloves and a handbag that's tidy inside and out all contribute to the impression of efficiency you want to make. If you can manage to look attractive as well it will help your interviewer to feel you'd be pleasant to have around.

Though anything goes in most offices these days, from sundresses to black stockings, it's safest to err on the formal side for an interview: gloves, high-heeled court shoes, dress and jacket, dress and coat, suit, or, in summer, a towny, fairly high-necked dress. The girl who breezes in in skirt and jumper and flat-heeled shoes may suggest that she will take her work as casually as she does her clothes. But it's quite unnecessary to wear a hat.

A popular fallacy is to suppose that you can dazzle a man into giving you a job. In fact, the femme fatale act of plunging necklines, masses of jewellery, scent and makeup will scare most men into not taking you on; their jobs depend on keeping their minds on their work, as well as on the efficiency of their subordinates.

And that means that the short-sighted girl should wear her glasses. If she blunders beautifully but blindly round the office she may get asked out to dinner, but she's unlikely to get the job.

REFERENCES

For many jobs references are not necessary. But if you think one is likely to be helpful, you can either ask for a written reference from your old employer when you leave his firm (the head of your school or training college if it's your first job) or you can ask if he'd mind if you gave his name as a reference, in which case your new employer can write to him or ring him up. Before giving anyone's name as a reference it's good manners to ask their permission.

A written reference should be handed to you in an unsealed

envelope and should say how long you've worked for the firm, what your work was and how well you did it.

Written references are not usually enclosed in a letter of application. They are either produced at an interview or sent afterwards; it's accepted practice to send copies in case the originals might get lost. If a prospective employer insists on being sent the originals, he's in honour bound to let you have them back.

THE NEWCOMER

The first few weeks as a junior in a new job are rather like being a new girl at school and it's not a good idea to throw your weight around and start off by suggesting a way of revolutionizing the office filing system or asking the boss out to lunch.

On your first day, someone should take you round the offices introducing you to the people you will have to deal with. As for the work, if you don't understand it, the first few weeks are the time to ask and keep on asking. No one expects a newcomer to grasp everything at once and it's far better to ask twice about something in the first week than to make an elementary mistake after you've been with the firm two months. Don't follow the example of the new junior in a magazine office who hid two pages because she was too frightened to ask what should be done with them!

Even though nobody else observes them, the new junior should stick to the office rules, arriving on the dot in the morning and taking no more than the allotted time off for lunch. Taking liberties with the rules is a VIP's privilege and anyone who is constantly late, even though her work may be good, is storing up trouble for herself.

Greetings

Saying good morning when you come in and goodnight when you leave is part of ordinary good manners. But it's not so easy to know what to do, if you are late one morning and find yourself sharing a lift with the directors. Should you start up a bright conversation? Or maintain a remote silence and hope they don't notice you? It's obviously unnecessary to do anything if you haven't met them. If you think they know who you are, my advice is to smile and say good morning and leave them to start any bright conversation.

When You are Unavoidably Late

There are times when you can't help being late, when you cut your finger instead of the bread or something goes wrong with the plumbing. When this happens you should either ring your superior yourself or get someone else to ring him. In the case of illness, if it lasts more than three days most firms ask for a note or certificate from your doctor.

Knocking on Doors

In a civilized firm nobody knocks on office doors unless they are going to see a VIP with whom they normally have very little to do. The only other time it would be good manners to knock is when something may be happening on the other side of the door that you're not supposed to hear. In this case, you can give a warning knock and enter without waiting for a 'Come in'; alternatively simply stick your head round the door and withdraw if you're obviously interrupting.

But the custom varies from firm to firm. If in yours everyone knocks on everyone else's door, genteel and unnecessary though this is, the most tactful course for a newcomer is to follow suit.

Lunch with a Colleague

The custom is for each to pay his or her own share.

Secretarial Manners

They shouldn't present any difficulty if you use common sense, tact and ordinary courtesy. Obviously your boss won't want to be interrupted in the middle of an interview except for a very good reason—if there is an important telephone call, a note on his desk is the best way to tell him.

What do you say if you're asked to collect a visitor from the waiting room? Something like this: 'Mr Smith? I'm Mr Adams' secretary. He asked me to show you to his office.' You lead the way, open the office door, say, 'Mr Smith for you,

Mr Adams,' stand aside to let the visitor pass and close the door behind him.

On the Telephone

The correct and time-saving thing to do, whether you're ringing or being rung up, is to announce your identity at once: 'Blenkins and Company', 'Mr Adams' secretary', or whatever is appropriate. A secretary should never put a call straight through to her boss; she should get the caller's name and ask him to wait a moment while she sees if her boss is in—even though he may be sitting at the next desk.

If you are in a position to ask a secretary to get someone on the phone for you, you shouldn't keep them waiting when they come on the line. All too commonly done, this is extremely tactless.

Personal Telephone Calls

Some firms don't allow them at all. Where they are allowed they should be kept to a minimum, since someone may be trying to get through on business and employees aren't paid to spend the morning quarrelling with their boy friends, or holding post mortems on last night's party.

Mistakes

Everyone makes them occasionally, and the only thing to do is to admit them at once while there is still time to put them right. Even if, when you discover your mistake, it's too late to do anything about it, it's better to tell your immediate superior than leave him to find out for himself.

Office Politics

Intrigues are part of the life of every firm. Mary thinks she should have had Jane's job and she is now busy stirring up all the hostility she can against Jane, trying to make the office so hot for her that she's forced to leave. However much you may sympathize with either Jane or Mary, the only wise course is to steer clear. Intrigues in an office may do enormous damage to the work output as well as creating a thoroughly unpleasant atmosphere, and sooner or later anyone who encourages them is out.

MEN IN THE OFFICE

As far as they're concerned you are simply a colleague. As soon as you enter the office you forfeit your feminine privileges. You do your own fetching and carrying, open your own doors and if you go out to lunch with them or for an after-work drink you will probably be expected to pay your share. If you ever come across a man who regards you as a woman first and a colleague second, beware before you plunge head-long and remember that if it comes to the point when you never want to see him again, you may have to resign your job.

THE OFFICE WOLF

Fortunately he is a rare phenomenon. But if your boss tells you one day that his wife doesn't understand him and follows this up with repeated invitations to dinner, there is obviously no respectable future for you in the firm and your only course is to hand in your resignation.

OFFICE COLLECTIONS

Collections for leaving and wedding presents are a feature of most firms. Ideally contributions should only be solicited from people who know the girl in question. But in fact, you may very well be asked to stump up for someone you've met once and will never meet again within two weeks of your start in a new job, and unless you are extremely strong-minded, you will fork out. How much do other people give? In a large firm, most people work on the principle that if everyone gives a little, the result will be quite a handsome present and the average contribution, except in the case of a personal friend, is between a shilling and two and six; the boss may feel he ought to give a bit more. As you fork out your lunch money for the umpteenth time, console yourself—if you can!—with the thought that your turn will come.

CHRISTMAS AND BIRTHDAY PRESENTS

Beyond possibly finding sixpence all round for a potted plant for the head of the department at Christmas time, no one in their right senses does anything about Christmas and birthday presents in the office. One present can so easily snowball into a tradition. Jane gives Mary a bottle of scent for her birthday, Mary feels she has to give Jane something on hers, and before the year's out, birthday presents all round have become office routine and a crippling expense for anyone on a small budget. More charitable to everybody in the long run is the curious custom that prevails in many firms for the girl whose birthday it is to buy a cake to hand round to her workmates.

OFFICE PARTIES AND OUTINGS

The snare here is to remember in the midst of all the informal jolly eating and drinking that the boss, however much he's letting his hair down, is still the boss and that jokes at his or the firm's expense that seem innocent enough in the hilarity of the moment may look different when recollected by him the next morning. One young man arriving at the office the following day found a note of dismissal on his desk.

Otherwise, manners at the firm's party should be the same as at any other party. You say goodbye and thank you to your host, unless he really doesn't know you're alive, or it's a very large party. Your men colleagues who, in the office, will happily watch while you struggle with an enormous pile of files, will spring into gallant action and expect to fetch and carry for you and light your cigarette.

BUSINESS LUNCHES

The woman who entertains people to lunch on behalf of her firm is an accepted part of the business scene today. Her guests expect her to pay, knowing that she will get her money back on expenses. But to save any possible embarrassment, many women have an account at the restaurant so that when the bill comes all they need do is sign it.

GIVING NOTICE

The correct way is by letter. But if you're on friendly terms with your immediate superior it's polite to tell him first. Good policy, too. It gives him an opportunity to offer you a better job than the one for which you are leaving.

RISES AND BONUSES

A routine rise or bonus arrives in your pay packet and you may or may not be expected to write and thank for it; different firms have different customs and the best course is to ask and do what the others do. In the case of a merit rise, the boss will call you in to tell you about it and will expect you to say thank you on the spot.

CHRISTIAN NAMES

In some newspaper offices everyone from the big chief to the secretaries is known to everyone else by his or her christian name. In one well-known London shop women who have worked beside each other for years still address each other as Miss Blank.

The best policy here is to do whatever your colleagues on the same level in the firm's hierarchy do or, if you're the junior in a department where everyone else is much older, call them by their surnames unless or until they ask you not to.

CHAPTER 5

TIPPING AND TRAVEL

WHATEVER ONE may think of the ethics of tipping, the livelihood of waiters, taxi-drivers and others is still to a large extent dependent on tips, which are considered part of their income by the tax authorities. Tip one must, and preferably, for one's pocket's sake, not along the lines of the girl who admitted: 'I always tip taxi-drivers more than I can afford because they do glare so!'

Deciding what to tip has never been more difficult than it is today when it is no longer possible to rely on the old comfortable standard of 10 per cent. While it is true to say that one should rarely give less there are many occasions when it is customary to give more, and anyone who sticks rigidly to the 10 per cent rule is going to meet if not with the offended tippees stock snub—'You need this more than I do!'—at least with a good many black looks.

The finer points of tipping depend on how rich you are and look. A prosperous business man is expected to give more than a young girl. Not that reality always comes up to expectations. Millionaires have been known to walk out of an expensive West End of London hotel without tipping a penny.

The suggested tips in this chapter are for people who don't want to be mean, but haven't got money to splash around.

TAXIS

Tip proportionately more on a small fare than on a large one, and more again if the taxi is held up by crowded streets or has to wait outside your house, as taxi metres work largely on mileage, not on time.

> On 2s fare tip 6d;
> on fares between 2s and 4s tip 9d;
> on a 4 or 5s fare, 1s;

on a 6s fare, 1s 3d;
on a 7s fare, 1s 6d;
on an 8s fare, 1s 9d;
on a 9s fare, 2s;
on a 10s fare, 2s 3d.

If you ask the driver to drive fast because you have a train to catch, 3s is not too much to tip on a 6s fare. If you take a taxi late at night or on Christmas Day, the driver will expect a larger than usual tip.

What to do if you have nothing less than a pound? Allow for the cost of the fare and the tip and, when you hand the note to the driver, ask him for so much change.

HIRED CARS WITH DRIVER

For an outing lasting four or five hours, tip on the Bentley, Rolls level 10s, correspondingly less for a smaller car. The driver of the car that takes members of a wedding party to the church and on to the reception afterwards expects 5s to 10s; 10s is usual in the West End of London. On an outing lasting a whole day tip £1; the driver will also expect to have his meals bought for him.

If you engage a taxi for a half or a whole day, it is usual to settle on a price with the driver beforehand, in which case he doesn't expect a tip on top.

TRAINS

Porters

Tip 1s for the first case, 6d for each piece after that. For a trunk, tip 1s 6d to 2s. Tip 2s 6d if your porter gets you a particular seat on the train as well as carrying one or two cases.

Restaurant Car

Tip the table waiter 10 to 12½ per cent of the bill unless a service charge is included when a tip of 2½ per cent is ample. The wine waiter is not tipped.

Sleeping Car Attendant

If you're travelling first class leave him 2s 6d on your morning tea and biscuits tray.

The stewardess is never tipped. In fact, no one should be tipped the plane side of the Customs. At airports in England and Scotland there is no need to tip the man who takes your baggage between car or bus and Customs as he's adequately paid for the job. At airports abroad airport porters expect to be tipped at the usual rate.

RESTAURANTS

Tip between 10 and 15 per cent depending on the quality of the restaurant, the size of the bill and the quality of the service. On a three pound bill in an expensive West End of London restaurant, the usual tip is 15 per cent, but on a ten pound bill, most people would consider 10 to 12½ per cent adequate. In a moderately priced restaurant, tip 10 to 12½ per cent.

In a licensed restaurant where cost of the drinks is included in the bill you tip your table waiter on the lot. You need tip the wine waiter only if you pay him for your drinks separately. In an unlicensed restaurant where the wine waiter has to go out to buy the wine, you give him the money for it before he goes, tip him out of the change when he comes back with the bottle, about 10 per cent of its cost.

COFFEE BARS

If the waitress brings the coffee to a table, most people would leave something under the saucer, 3*d* or 6*d* for two coffees.

DRINKS

In a pub you tip only if the drinks are brought to you at a table, about 6*d* for two drinks, 1*s* for a round costing 10*s*. But at the bar of a Ritz-level hotel, you do tip, not less than 1*s*; after that on a 10 per cent basis.

AT THE HAIRDRESSERS

Tip the girl who shampoos your hair 1*s*, 2*s* if you have a bleach or a perm which involves washing your hair twice. On a shampoo and set costing between 9*s* and 13*s* 6*d* tip your hairdresser 2*s* 6*d*; on a shampoo and set costing between 14*s* and £1, tip 3s or 3s 6d; on a bleach costing 30s, tip 4s or 4s 6d; on a perm costing £2, tip 5s. If the price is more, tip more. But if your hairdresser is the proprietor of the salon you're not expected to tip him. Usual tip to the manicurist is 1s.

CHRISTMAS BOXES

Tradesmen who call regularly—milkman, postman, dustman, laundryman, paper boy, coalman, etc—expect to be given a Christmas box the last time they call before Christmas. People tip according to their means; the larger the house and the more expensive the area, the more people feel obliged to give. Usual tips vary between 2s 6d and 10s. But at the large country house level tips may be as much as £2 each to milkman and postman.

CLOAKROOMS

The safest guide is to see what, if anything, other people have put in the saucer. Usual tip for leaving a coat at a theatre, hotel or reception rooms is 6d, 1s at a Ritz-level hotel.

WEEKEND STAY IN A HOUSE WITH STAFF

What most people tip varies between 5s and £1 depending on who they are, how much extra work their stay has caused and the grandness of the household. £1 is generous, 10s is usual—this is the sum normally left by a debutante on her dressing table for the living-in-maid who does her room. Where the help is not on such a grand scale, 5s is gratefully received. A young girl is not expected to tip men servants but an older woman normally would tip the butler. The cook, unless she does other things in the house as well, is not tipped, nor are gardeners. Chauffeurs are rarely tipped. There is no need to tip any member of the staff who doesn't do anything for you.

Nanny, of course, is never tipped.

WORKMEN IN THE HOME

Plumbers, electricians, decorators, window-cleaners, chimney sweeps, etc, are not normally tipped. But if the job's a long one they appreciate a cup of tea or a glass of beer.

REMOVAL MEN

They are usually tipped if the job involves moving heavy furniture up or down stairs according to how long the job takes and how difficult it is. The van driver who delivers a piece of furniture or a new carpet doesn't expect a tip if he leaves it in the hall, but he is usually tipped if he carries it up several flights of stairs—not less than 1s.

IN GARAGES

As a rule people don't tip for petrol only, but give a small tip, 6d or 9d, for any extra service, such as having the windscreen cleaned or their tyres pumped up.

HOTELS

How to Book

Make it absolutely clear what sort of accommodation you want, who you want it for and how long you are going to stay. If you want a quiet room with two single beds, say so, or you may find you have booked yourself a room with a double bed overlooking a noisy street. If you are bringing children, mention their ages as some hotels don't accept them under a certain age. If you have a dog, say what kind he is. Some hotels don't allow dogs at all; others have their own regulations as to size of dog and where in the hotel he is allowed.

It is also important to say whether you want all meals or just bed and breakfast. Many seaside resort hotels have a weekly price inclusive of all meals except afternoon tea— which is considerably cheaper than paying for each meal separately. Any special arrangement for children's diet should also be made in advance.

You should also check the price of the accommodation. This often varies according to the time of year.

Letters are usually addressed to the manager of the hotel. When you are informed that the accommodation you want is available, write back and book. In case of error, it's a good idea to repeat the details:

Dear Sir,

Thank you for your letter of the 26th June.

I should like to reserve the one double room with twin beds and a private bathroom and the adjoining single room, from June 1st to 31st at £– –s each per week, including breakfast and dinner.

Yours faithfully,

If you want accommodation in a hurry hotels will accept booking by telegram and usually by telephone. But however you book warn the hotel if you're likely to arrive late in the evening or you may find when you arrive, travel-worn and longing for bed at eleven o'clock at night, that your coming has been despaired of and your room let to someone else.

Luxury Hotels

A uniformed commissionaire stands outside the door. The hall is stiff with liveried pages and porters. Many people, used to homes where Mum is cook, chambermaid and porter as well, find their first sight of this grand establishment alarming. Used to doing all their own fetching and carrying, suddenly they step into a world where they aren't expected to lift a finger for themselves. In the face of this grandeur there is only one way to behave, as though you're used to it, from the start. When your taxi draws up at the hotel doors, wait for someone to come and take your cases. If no one comes, go into the hotel and ask one of the porters to bring them in. However light your cases, you will be starting off on the wrong foot if you carry them into the hall yourself. Inside the hotel you go straight up to the reception desk, find out the number of your room and register. The key will then be given to a porter who will carry your cases and show you up to your room.

Service

One of the problems of staying in a luxury hotel is whom should you ask to do what.

If you want food or drink brought up to your room, ask for room service or press the button on your telephone marked waiter.

If you want your husband's suit pressed, ask for the valet.

If you want your shoes cleaned, leave them outside your door last thing at night and they'll be ready waiting for you there the next morning. (This goes for most small hotels as well.)

If you want anything fetched or carried, suitcases taken downstairs or a newspaper brought up, get in touch with the hall porter; he is in charge of both porters and pages.

If you want anything in the middle of the night, phone the night porter.

If you want a hot water bottle or a clean towel, ring for the chambermaid.

If you want theatre tickets, there may be a special desk; if not, the hall porter may arrange them for you.

In a big hotel, the porter usually keeps a list of people who want to be called in the morning, in a smaller hotel the list is kept at the reception desk.

But the organization of different hotels does vary. Whenever you are in doubt as to whom to ask to do what you can always ring reception and get them to put you on to the right department. The receptionists are also the people to ask if you want to stay on an extra night, if you want your bill or if you want to know anything about the layout of the hotel.

Valuables

These should be handed in at the reception desk for safe keeping during your stay. Room keys are also left at the reception desk at small hotels, with the porter in larger hotels.

In the Dining Room

When you go in for the first time, you wait by the door for the head waiter to come up to you and show you to your table. As a rule the head waiter does none of the actual waiting. He takes your order, passes it on to the table waiter, arranges the seating and sees that everything runs smoothly.

The table you are given at your first meal is generally yours for the rest of your stay.

Visiting Someone in a Hotel

At a grand hotel you give the name of the person you have come to see to the hall porter, who will then ring your friend's room to see if he is there. If not, he will send a page to look for him. The page stands in the doorway of the hotel's public rooms and shouts: 'Paging Mr So and so.' If Mr So and so is found he will tip the page. Otherwise the visitor should tip the page when he returns to the hall.

In a smaller hotel you contact the person you have come to see through the receptionist.

Leaving

It is a hotel rule that guests must vacate their rooms by twelve midday on the day they are leaving. But if you ask the receptionist or the hall porter you can arrange to have your cases kept in the hotel until you want to collect them.

You are not expected to carry your own cases downstairs!

Tipping

A generally agreed fair proportion of the bill to divide among the staff who have done anything for you is 10 per cent for a week's stay, more for just a couple of nights, less for a fortnight's stay.

Distributing this in a small hotel is simple. If you eat regularly in the dining room give half your 10 per cent to your table waiter, distribute the other half between your chambermaid and the porter who carries your cases. If you have breakfast only in the dining room, the chambermaid should, of course, get a larger share.

Tipping in a luxury hotel bristling with liveried staff all looking as though they expected largesse is far more complex. And the chances are that after a first stay in a hotel of this kind, when the hotel door finally swings to behind you, you will feel a twinge of guilt. Should you have tipped the door-man and the lift boy? Did you leave the chambermaid enough?

Your chambermaid and table waiter are always tipped at the end of your stay. Though some people do tip the head waiter as well there is no need to, as waiters' tips go into a pool and he will get his share.

Porters and pages are tipped at the time they do anything for you, pages 6d or 1s according to the errand and the hotel, porters not less than 1s 6d for two light cases at a grand commercial hotel, or 2s 6d at the Ritz level. Floor waiters may be tipped either at the time they do anything for you, about 1s for breakfast in bed at a grand commercial hotel, or, if you give them a lot of work, at the end of your stay.

Though some people tip the head porter, at the end of their stay, there is no need to tip him unless he does anything extra for you. If you do tip him, you can't very well give him less than 5s at a grand commercial hotel, or 10s at the Ritz level. The barman may be tipped either per round or at the end of your stay, 10 to 12 per cent of your drinks bill. The waiter who brings you coffee in the lounge is tipped 6d or 1s, depending on the hotel. The doorman is tipped when he gets you a taxi, about 6d at a grand commercial hotel, 1s at the Ritz level. Whether you tip doorman and lift boy a few shillings when you leave is up to you. Some people do; some people don't.

In the majority of hotels where a service charge is added to the bill, porters and pages still expect to be tipped, and most people still leave their chambermaid and table waiter a little, but don't tip otherwise except for extra service.

But in Trust Houses where a service charge is added to the bill, this is fairly divided between the staff, and there is no need to tip any of them at all unless they do something for you right outside their normal duties.

On Board Ship

In most ships each class has its own separate quarters, deck, dining rooms, lounges, even dances and film shows, so you practically never meet anyone travelling by a different class.

The only members of the crew passengers have much to do with are the purser and the stewards.

The Purser

He deals with any complaints about cabins, takes names for shore trips, changes your money and will look after valuables, passports, documents, etc.

In the Cabin

The cabin steward keeps your cabin clean; the cabin stewardess makes the bed. You can also ask them to bring you breakfast in bed, take your clothes to the ship's laundry, see what's happened to your cabin luggage if it's not there when you get aboard, and to get your luggage marked 'Wanted on board' from the luggage room. (Luggage marked 'Not wanted on board' goes in the hold and you can't get at it until the ship finally docks.)

In the Dining Room

The dining room steward arranges the seating. If you have any special preference as to where you would like to sit and with whom, you can usually arrange this with him on the first evening. You sit at the same table throughout the trip unless you ask to be moved or the captain suddenly discovers you are a brilliant raconteur and invites you to join his party. The captain's table is the place of honour, where the most important first class passengers are invited to sit—though the prettiest girl on board is also likely to find her way there!

On Deck

The deck steward sets the chairs out every morning and brings them in at night; he also brings out and sets up the deck games. If you want to make sure you sit on a certain part of the deck—the off-shore side is the coolest on a voyage through the tropics—or next a handsome millionaire, you can rent a deck chair from the deck steward and arrange to have it put in a particular spot. That chair and that spot are yours for the rest of the trip. The time to see the deck steward is on the first evening—he is usually to be found on deck.

On long voyages passengers form a games committee which organizes various deck game tournaments. Competitors are charged an entrance fee which pays for prizes bought at the ship's shop.

Clothes

Daytime clothes are casual, slacks, skirts and sweaters, and shorts in hot weather. A warm and windproof jacket or coat is essential. On ships that have more than one class, first class passengers change for dinner, men into dinner jackets, women into cocktail or short evening dresses. Long dresses are rarely worn. In tourist and cabin classes—and in some first class only ships—most men wear lounge suits for dinner, dinner jackets only on gala nights.

Nobody changes for the religious service on Sundays.

What You Pay For

All meals on board, including breakfast in bed, are included in the price of the ticket. But you pay for your drinks, cigarettes, anything you buy in the shop, your laundry and, of course, for any appointments at the hairdresser's or beauty salon.

Organized shore trips also cost extra.

Tipping on a Ship

What people tip on ships varies enormously. It depends on the luxuriousness of the ship, what class you are travelling, what accommodation you have, what the service is like, how many of the stewards you come in contact with, and who you are. If you have a private bathroom, you are expected to tip more than if you haven't. A young girl is not expected to tip as much as a business man travelling on an expense account. If you don't use the bar, smoke room or lounge, there is no need to tip bar, smoke room or lounge stewards. The list of tips given below is intended as a guide only and not a hard and fast rule.

Tips are proportionately larger on a short voyage than on a long one. A single person tips proportionately more than a couple. The biggest tips usually go to the cabin and dining room stewards. But if your cabin stewardess does a lot of work for you, you would tip her at the same rate as your cabin steward.

On a Four Day trans-Atlantic Voyage in a Luxury Liner
First Class:

Cabin Steward: £2 10s to £3 for a single person, £4 or £5 for a couple.

Cabin Stewardess: Not less than £1 for a couple.

Dining Room Steward: £2 10s or £3 for a single person, £4 or £5 for a couple.

Head Dining Room Steward: Not less than £1 if he gives you special attention.

Bar Steward: 10 per cent of the cost of your drinks—at the end of the trip if they are put on your bill, otherwise tip per round.

Bathroom Steward: 10s if you use him.

Deck Steward: 15s or £1 for one or two people. If you spend all your time being ill in your cabin or drinking at the bar, of course you don't tip him at all.

The Boots: A few shillings if you use him.

Cabin Class:

Cabin Steward: 30s for a single person, £2 for a couple. Or divide this between your cabin steward and stewardess.

Dining Room Steward: 30s for a single person, £2 for a couple.

Bar Steward: 10 per cent of the cost of your drinks.

Bathroom Steward: 7s 6d.

Deck Steward: 10s.

Tourist Class:

Cabin Steward: £1 for a single person, 30s for a couple. Or divide this between your cabin steward and stewardess.

Dining Room Steward: £1 for a single person, 30s for a couple.

Bar Steward: 10 per cent of the cost of your drinks.

Bathroom Steward: 5s.

Deck Steward: 10s.

On a Sea Voyage Lasting Two to Three Weeks

First Class:

Cabin Steward: £3 to £5 for a single person, £4 to £7 for a couple.

Stewardess: £1 or 30s if all she does is make the beds.

Dining Room Steward: £3 to £5 for a single person, £4 to £7 for a couple.

Head Dining Room Steward: Not less than £1 if he gives you special attention.

Bar Steward: 10 per cent of the cost of your drinks.

Bathroom Steward: £1 for a couple.

Deck Steward: £2.

Other Stewards: Tip the ones who have been most useful to you, from 10s each.

The Boots: A few shillings, according to use.

In a ship where stewards are not tipped individually and passengers instead contribute to a pool, £10 is the minimum for a single person travelling first class on a two to three weeks' voyage.

Tourist Class

Passengers travelling this class tend to give what they can afford rather than what they feel is expected of them. But half to two thirds of the first class rate of tipping is fair.

On a Cruise

Tip as for a sea voyage.

When to Tip

With the exception of hairdressers, who are tipped on the spot at the same rate as on land, and the man who brings your drinks if they're not added to your bill, all tips should be given at the end of the voyage. Flamboyant tippers who offer stewards half a five pound note at the beginning of the journey with the promise that the other half will be forthcoming at Southampton are not popular with other passengers.

TIPPING ON THE CONTINENT

From the tipping point of view the easiest countries are the communist ones where it is considered a degrading capitalist habit, though in Moscow now taxi-drivers are sufficiently 'degraded' to accept the odd gratuity from tourists. In Yugoslavia taxi-drivers are tipped—10 per cent—but nobody else. Next easiest group of countries are the Scandinavian where comparatively little tipping goes on. But in the rest of Europe the 'degrading capitalist practice' is still with us—and very confusing it is, since whom to tip varies from country to country.

In Hotels

A service charge is usually included in the bill. It's not necessary to tip except for extra service, though many people leave a small tip for the chambermaid. If a service charge is not included, tip 12 to 15 per cent.

In Restaurants

A service charge is usually included. Whether you tip a little on top of this is up to you. In a first class restaurant in France it is usual to tip the wine waiter. If no service charge is included, tip your table waiter 12 to 15 per cent, depending on the quality of the service.

In Theatres and Cinemas

Both cinema and theatre usherettes are generally tipped in France, Italy, Portugal, Belgium and Spain. In Holland you please yourself whether or not you tip the usherette. There is no need to tip usherettes in Greece, Denmark, Switzerland, Norway, Sweden, Austria, Germany or Finland.

Taxi-drivers

In Norway and Finland they don't expect a tip. In Germany they expect small change only, in Spain not more than 10 per cent. Elsewhere tip as in England.

Railway Porters

In most countries there is a fixed tariff. But in Spain where this is very meagre, it's usual to give more, not less than 5 pesetas per piece. Where there is no fixed tariff, tip as in England.

At Garages

It is usual to give a small tip even if you are only filling up with petrol, except in Denmark, Norway, Sweden, Holland and Finland.

CHAPTER 6

TITLES

How to Address Peers, Baronets and Knights

The growing tendency towards informality and the feeling these days that a man should be honoured for his own achievements rather than those of his ancestors has made practically obsolete some of the traditional ways of addressing titled people. The styles listed under 'Formal Modes of Address' in this chapter are rarely used today except by employees and people on a much lower social level. The old-fashioned formal way to end a letter: 'I have the honour to be your obedient servant', etc, is practically never used now except when writing to members of the royal family, 'Yours faithfully' or 'Yours truly' being commonly used instead.

Envelopes of business letters are now usually addressed in the same way as envelopes for social letters.

The peers are, in order of precedence, Dukes, Marquesses, Earls, Viscounts and Barons.

Duke

(For Royal Dukes see chapter on Royalty)

Social Forms of Address

In Speech: Introduce him as 'The Duke of ——', refer to him as 'The Duke', or 'The Duke of ——', address him as 'Duke'.

In Writing: Begin, 'Dear Duke of ——' or, if you know him fairly well, 'Dear Duke'. Address the envelope 'His Grace, The Duke of ——' or 'The Duke of ——'.

Formal Modes of Address

In Speech: Refer to him as 'His Grace', address him as 'Your Grace'.

In Writing: Begin, 'My Lord Duke'.

Duchess

Social Forms of Address

In Speech: Introduce her as 'The Duchess of ——', refer to her as 'The Duchess of ——' or 'The Duchess'. Address her as 'Duchess'.

In Writing: Begin, 'Dear Duchess of ——' or 'Dear Duchess'. Address the envelope 'Her Grace, The Duchess of ——' or 'The Duchess of ——'.

Formal Modes of Address

In Speech: Refer to her as 'Her Grace', address her as 'Your Grace'.

In Writing: Begin, 'Madam' or 'Your Grace'.

Marquess

Social Forms of Address

In Speech: Introduce him, refer to him and address him as 'Lord (Leicestershire)'.

In Writing: Begin 'Dear Marquess (of Leicestershire)' or 'Dear Lord (Leicestershire)'. Address the envelope 'The Marquess (of Leicestershire)'.

Formal Modes of Address

In Speech: Refer to him as 'His Lordship', address him as 'My Lord' or 'Your Lordship'.

In Writing: Begin, 'My Lord'.

Marchioness

Social Forms of Address

In Speech: Introduce her, refer to her and address her as Lady (Leicestershire).

In Writing: Begin, 'Dear Marchioness (of Leicestershire) or 'Dear Lady (Leicestershire)'. Address the envelope 'The Marchioness (of Leicestershire)'.

Formal Modes of Address

In Speech: Address her as 'Madam' or 'Your Ladyship'.

Refer to her as 'Her Ladyship'.
In Writing: Begin, 'Madam'.

Earl

Social Forms of Address

In Speech: Introduce him, refer to him and address him as 'Lord (Wallingford)'.

In Writing: Begin, 'Dear Earl (of Wallingford)' or 'Dear Lord (Wallingford)'. Address the envelope 'The Earl (of Wallingford)'.

Formal Modes of Address

Same as for Marquess.

Countess

Social Forms of Address

In Speech: Introduce her, refer to her and address her as 'Lady (Wallingford)'.

In Writing: Begin, 'Dear Countess (of Wallingford)' or 'Dear Lady (Wallingford)'. Address the envelope 'The Countess (of Wallingford)'.

Formal Modes of Address

Same as for Marchioness.

Viscount

Social Forms of Address

In Speech: Introduce him, refer to him and address him as 'Lord (Bellingham)'.

In Writing: Begin, 'Dear Viscount (Bellingham)' or 'Dear Lord (Bellingham)'. Address the envelope 'The Viscount (Bellingham)'.

Formal Modes of Address

Same as for Marquess.

Viscountess

Social Forms of Address

In Speech: Introduce her, refer to her and address her as 'Lady (Bellingham)'.

In Writing: Begin, 'Dear Viscountess (Bellingham)' or 'Dear Lady (Bellingham)'. Address the envelope 'The Viscountess (Bellingham)'.

Formal Modes of Address

Same as for Marchioness.

Baron

Social Forms of Address

In Speech: Introduce him, refer to him and address him as 'Lord (Inchworth)'.

In Writing: Begin, 'Dear Lord (Inchworth)'. Address the envelope 'The Lord (Inchworth)'.

Formal Modes of Address

Same as for Marquess.

Baroness

Social Forms of Address

In Speech: Introduce her, refer to her and address her as 'Lady (Inchworth)'.

In Writing: Begin, 'Dear Lady (Inchworth)'. Address the envelope 'The Lady (Inchworth)'.

Formal Modes of Address

Same as for Marchioness.

Eldest Son of Duke, Marquess or Earl

He bears by courtesy his father's second title. Thus the eldest son of a Duke may be a Marquess, the eldest son of a Marquess may be an Earl and the eldest son of an Earl may be a Viscount. They and their wives are addressed in all respects as though their titles were 'actual' instead of 'courtesy' except that they should strictly speaking be addressed on envelopes without the prefix 'The'. Thus the son of a Duke who bears the courtesy title 'Marquess of X' should be addressed on an envelope simply as 'Marquess of X'.

Eldest Grandson of a Duke or a Marquess

He bears by courtesy his grandfather's third title. Thus the grandson of a Duke may be an Earl and the grandson of a Marquess a Viscount. They and their wives are addressed in all respects as though their titles were 'actual' except that strictly speaking they should be addressed without the prefix 'The' on envelopes.

Younger Son of Duke or Marquess

Social Forms of Address

In Speech: Introduce him as 'Lord (John Smith)', refer to him as 'Lord (John Smith)' or 'Lord (John)', address him as 'Lord (John)'.

In Writing: Begin, 'Dear Lord (John Smith)' or if the acquaintance is more than slight, 'Dear Lord (John)'. Address the envelope 'Lord (John Smith)'.

Formal Modes of Address

Same as for Marquess.

Wife of Younger Son of Duke or Marquess

Social Forms of Address

In Speech: Introduce her as 'Lady (John Smith)', refer to her as 'Lady (John Smith)' or 'Lady John'. Address her as 'Lady (John)'.

In Writing: Begin, 'Dear Lady (John Smith)' or if the acquaintance is more than slight 'Dear Lady (John)'. Address the envelope 'Lady (John Smith)'.

Formal Modes of Address

Same as for Marchioness.

Unmarried Daughter of Duke, Marquess or Earl

Social Forms of Address

> *In Speech:* Introduce her as 'Lady (Mary Jones)', refer to her as 'Lady (Mary Jones)' or 'Lady (Mary)'. Address her as 'Lady (Mary)'.
>
> *In Writing:* Begin, 'Dear Lady (Mary Jones)' or if the acquaintance is more than slight 'Dear Lady (Mary)'. Address the envelope 'Lady (Mary Jones)'.

Formal Modes of Address

Same as for Marchioness.

Married Daughter of Duke or Marquess

If she marries a peer (*ie* the owner of an actual, not a courtesy, title) she is addressed according to the rank of her husband, also if she marries the eldest son of a Duke or a Marquess.

If she marries anyone else, she keeps her own title 'Lady (Mary)'. Thus if she married the eldest son of an Earl with the courtesy title of Viscount X, she would be known as Lady Mary X (though occasionally if she marries the eldest son of an Earl she may drop her own title and be addressed according to her husband's courtesy title). If she married the younger son of a Duke or a Marquess, 'Lord John Smith', she would be known as 'Lady Mary Smith'. If she married the younger son of an Earl or the son of a Viscount or Baron, 'Hon. Jeremy Brown', she would be known as Lady Mary Brown. If she married a Baronet or a Knight, 'Sir George South', she would be known as 'Lady Mary South'. If she married plain 'Mr Paul West', she would be known as 'Lady Mary West'. Except that she no longer uses her maiden name, she is addressed in the same way as an unmarried daughter of a Duke or Marquess.

Married Daughter of an Earl

If she marries an Earl's eldest son, she is addressed according to his rank, otherwise correct modes of address are the same as for married daughters of Dukes and Marquesses.

Younger Son of Earl, Son of Viscount or Baron

Social Forms of Address

In Speech: Introduce him, refer to him and address him as 'Mr (North)'.

In Writing: Begin, 'Dear Mr (North)'. Address the envelope 'Hon. (Alan North)' ('The' before Hon. is often used but it is no longer considered strictly correct.)

Formal Modes of Address

In Speech: Refer to him as 'Mr (North)', address him as 'Sir'.

In Writing: Begin, 'Sir'.

Wife of Above

Social Forms of Address

In Speech: Introduce her, refer to her and address her as 'Mrs (North)'.

In Writing: Begin, 'Dear Mrs (North)'. Address the envelope 'Hon. Mrs (Alan North)'.

Formal Modes of Address

In Speech: Refer to her as 'Mrs (North)'. Address her as 'Madam'.

In Writing: Begin, 'Madam'.

Unmarried Daughter of Viscount or Baron

Social Forms of Address

In Speech: Introduce her, refer to her and address her as 'Miss (North)'.

In Writing: Begin, 'Dear Miss (North)'. Address the envelope 'Hon. (Anne North)'.

Formal Modes of Address

Refer to her as 'Miss (North)'. Otherwise as for wives of Younger Sons of Earls.

Married Daughter of Viscount or Baron

In Speech: According to the rank of her husband.

In Writing: Begin according to rank of her husband. On envelopes: According to her husband's rank if she marries a man of equal or higher rank than herself. If she marries a man of lower rank she keeps her own title. Thus if she marries a baronet or a knight, she is addressed as 'Hon. Lady (Kinley)'. If she marries a commoner as 'Hon. Mrs (Ffoulks)'.

Widow of Peer or Baronet

The general custom is to address her in the same way as when her husband was alive unless the present peer or baronet is married, in which event her own christian name is usually used in front of the title, on envelopes 'Henrietta, Duchess of X', 'Henrietta, Lady X', etc. But if she is the senior widow, she may prefer to be styled, 'The Dowager Duchess of X', 'The Dowager Lady X', etc. In speech and at the beginning of letters she is addressed as if her husband were still alive. If she marries again, she loses any title gained by her previous marriage.

Divorced Wife of Peer or Baronet

She is styled 'Henrietta, Duchess of ——', etc, unless she remarries in which case she loses any title gained by her previous marriage.

Baronet

Social Forms of Address

In Speech: Introduce him as 'Sir (Donald Kinley)', refer to him as 'Sir (Donald Kinley)' or 'Sir (Donald)', address him as 'Sir (Donald)'.

In Writing: Begin, 'Dear Sir (Donald Kinley)' or, if the acquaintance is more than slight, 'Dear Sir (Donald)'. Address the envelope 'Sir (Donald Kinley), Bt'.

Formal Modes of Address

In Speech: Refer to him as 'Sir (Donald Kinley)', address him as 'Sir'.

In Writing: Begin, 'Sir'.

Social Forms of Address

   In Speech: 'Lady (Kinley)'.

   In Writing: Begin, 'Dear Lady (Kinley)'. Address the envelope 'Lady (Kinley)'.

Formal Modes of Address

   Same as for Marchioness.

Knight

In the case of a knight of an order you must give him the appropriate letters after his name on an envelope, *eg* Sir (Alexander Williams) KBE, CMG. In the case of a knight bachelor, he may be addressed simply as 'Sir (Alexander Williams)'. Otherwise knights are addressed in the same way as Baronets.

Wife of a Knight

In the same way as for Baronet's wife.

Dame

Social Forms of Address

   In Speech: Introduce her as 'Dame (Margaret Green)'. Refer to her as 'Dame (Margaret Green)' or 'Dame (Margaret)'. Address her as 'Dame (Margaret)'.

   In Writing: Begin, 'Dear Dame (Margaret Green)' or 'Dear Dame (Margaret)'. The appropriate letters should always be added after her name on an envelope *eg* 'Dame (Margaret Green) GBE'.

Formal Modes of Address

   In Speech: Refer to her as 'Dame (Margaret Green)'. Address her as 'Madam'.

   In Writing: Begin, 'Dear Madam'.

THE CHURCH OF ENGLAND

Archbishop

In Speech: Introduce him as 'the Archbishop of ——', refer to him as 'the Archbishop of ——' or as 'the Archbishop'. Address him as 'Your Grace', both formally and socially or, if you're on very friendly terms, as 'Archbishop'.

In Writing: In a formal letter begin 'My Lord Archbishop' or 'Your Grace'. In an informal letter begin 'Dear Lord Archbishop' or, if you're on very friendly terms, 'Dear Archbishop'. Address the envelope, 'His Grace The Lord Archbishop of ——'.

Bishop

In Speech: Introduce him as 'the Bishop of ——', refer to him as 'His Lordship', address him as 'My Lord', both formally and socially. People on familiar terms with him may address him as 'Bishop'.

In Writing: In a formal letter begin, 'My Lord' or 'My Lord Bishop'. In an informal letter begin 'Dear Lord Bishop', or more familiarly, 'Dear Bishop'. Address the envelope, 'The Right Rev. The Lord Bishop of ——' except when writing to the Bishop of Meath who is addressed as 'The Most Rev.'.

Conventionally these modes of address are used for suffragan and overseas bishops as well as diocesan.

Dean and Provost

In Speech: Introduce him as 'the Dean of ——' or 'the Provost of ——', address him as 'Mr Dean' or 'Mr Provost'.

In Writing: In a formal letter begin, 'Very Rev. Sir'. In a social letter begin 'Dear Mr Dean' or 'Dear Mr Provost'. Address the envelope 'The Very Rev. The Dean (or Provost) of ——'.

Archdeacon

In Speech: Introduce him and refer to him as 'the Archdeacon of ——'. Address him as 'Mr Archdeacon'.

In Writing: In a formal letter begin, 'Venerable Sir'. In a social letter begin 'Dear Mr Archdeacon'. Address the envelope 'The Venerable The Archdeacon of ——'.

81

Canon and Prebendary

In Speech: Introduce him, refer to him and address him as 'Canon (Smith)' or 'Prebendary (Smith)'.

In Writing: In a formal letter begin 'Reverend Sir'. In a social letter begin 'Dear Canon (Smith)' or 'Dear Prebendary (Smith)'. Address the envelope 'The Rev. Canon (or Prebendary) J. Smith'.

Minor Canons, Rural Deans and other Clergy

In Speech and Letters: Introduce, refer to and address them as 'Mr Smith' (never as 'The Reverend' or 'the Reverend Smith'). Envelopes are addressed 'The Rev. (J. Smith)'.

Wives of Clergy

Address them as plain 'Mrs', unless either they or their husbands have a secular title, in which case the normal rules apply.

THE NAVY

Admiral of the Fleet

Address the envelope, 'Admiral of the Fleet, (Sir John Smith)'. Otherwise address him according to his peerage or other rank.

Admiral, Vice Admiral, Rear Admiral

In Speech: Introduce him as 'Admiral (Smith)' or if he is a knight or baronet as 'Admiral (Sir George Smith)'. Address him as 'Admiral (Smith)' or if he is a knight or baronet as 'Sir (George)'.

In Writing: Begin, 'Dear Admiral (Smith)', 'Dear Admiral' or if he is a knight or baronet, 'Dear Sir (George)'. It is correct to give him his full title on the envelope 'Admiral (Sir George Smith)', 'Vice Admiral (Sir George Smith)', 'Rear Admiral (A. E. Smith)', though socially the 'Vice' or 'Rear' is often omitted.

Commodore

In Speech: Introduce and address him as 'Commodore (Smith)'.

In Writing: Begin, 'Dear Commodore (Smith)'. Address the envelope 'Commodore (J. N. Smith)'.

Captain

In Speech: Introduce and address him as 'Captain (Smith)'.
In Writing: Begin, 'Dear Captain Smith'. Address the envelope 'Captain (J. N. Smith, DSO), RN'.

Commander

In Speech: Introduce and address him as 'Commander (Smith)'.
In Writing: Begin, 'Dear Commander (Smith)'. Address the envelope 'Commander (J. N. Smith) RN'.

Lieutenant Commander

In Speech: Introduce and address him as 'Lieutenant Commander (Smith)'.
In Writing: Begin, 'Dear Lieutenant Commander (Smith)'. Address the envelope 'Lieut-Commander (J. N. Smith) RN'.

Lieutenant

In Speech: Address him as 'Lieutenant (Smith)'.
In Writing: Begin, 'Dear Lieutenant (Smith)'. Address the envelope 'Lieutenant (J. N. Smith) RN'.

Sub-Lieutenant

In Speech: Address him as 'Mr (Smith)'.
In Writing: Begin, 'Dear Mr (Smith)'. Address the envelope 'Sub-Lieutenant (J. N. Smith) RN'.

Midshipman

In Speech: Address him as 'Mr (Smith)'.
In Writing: Begin, 'Dear Mr (Smith)'. Address the envelope either 'Midshipman (J. N. Smith) RN' or '(J. N. Smith) Esq. RN'.

Cadet

In Speech: Address him as 'Mr (Smith)'.
In Writing: Begin, 'Dear Mr (Smith)'. Address the envelope '(J. N. Smith) Esq. RN'.

Field-Marshal

Address the envelope, 'Field-Marshal (Lord ——)'. Otherwise address him according to his peerage or other rank.

General, Lieutenant-General, Major General

In Speech: Introduce him as 'General (Smith)' or if he is a knight or baronet, 'General Sir (George Smith)'. Address him as 'General Smith' or 'Sir (George)'.

In Writing: Begin, 'Dear General (Smith)' or 'Dear Sir (George)'. It is correct to address the envelope 'General (Sir George Smith)', 'Lieut-General (Sir George Smith)', 'Major General (J. N. Smith)'. Though socially Lieutenant and Major are often omitted.

Brigadier

In Speech: Address him as 'Brigadier (Smith)'.

In Writing: Address the envelope 'Brigadier (J. N. Smith)'.

Colonel

In Speech: Address him as 'Colonel (Smith)'.

In Writing: Address the envelope 'Colonel (A. E. Smith)'.

Lieutenant-Colonel

In Speech: Address him as 'Colonel (Smith)'.

In Writing: Begin, 'Dear Colonel (Smith)'. Address the envelope 'Lieut-Colonel (J. N. Smith)'. The regiment is added after the name preceded by any decorations.

Major

In Speech: Address him as 'Major (Smith)'.

In Writing: Begin, 'Dear Major (Smith)'. Address the envelope 'Major (J. N. Smith)' (name of regiment).

Captain

In Speech: Address him as 'Captain (Smith)'.

In Writing: Begin, 'Dear Captain (Smith)'. Address the envelope 'Captain (J. N. Smith)' (name of regiment).

Lieutenant and Second Lieutenant

In Speech: Address him as 'Mr (Smith)'.

In Writing: Address the envelope '(J. N. Smith) Esq.' (name of regiment). His rank is used only on official and service envelopes.

THE ROYAL AIR FORCE

Marshal of the Royal Air Force

Address the envelope 'Marshal of the Royal Air Force, (Lord ——)'. Otherwise address him as for his peerage or other rank.

Air Chief Marshal

In Speech: Introduce him as 'Air Chief Marshal (Sir Alan Smith)'. If he is a knight or a baronet, address him as 'Sir (Alan)'.

In Writing: Begin, 'Dear (Sir Alan)'. Address the envelope 'Air Chief Marshal (Sir Alan Smith)'.

Air Marshal

In Speech: Introduce him as 'Air Marshal (Smith)' or if a knight or baronet, 'Air Marshal Sir (Alan Smith)'. Address him as 'Air Marshal (Smith)' or 'Sir (Alan)'.

In Writing: Begin, 'Dear Air Marshal (Smith)' or 'Dear (Sir Alan)'. Address the envelope 'Air Marshal (A. E. Smith)' or 'Air Marshal (Sir Alan Smith)'.

Air Vice Marshal

In Speech: Introduce him as 'Air Vice Marshal (Smith)' or 'Air Vice Marshal (Sir Alan Smith)'. Address him as 'Air Vice Marshal (Smith)' or 'Sir (Alan)'.

In Writing: Begin, 'Dear Air Vice Marshal (Smith)' or 'Dear (Sir Alan)'. Address the envelope 'Air Vice Marshal (A. E. Smith)' or 'Air Vice Marshal (Sir Alan Smith)'.

Air Commodore

In Speech: Introduce him and address him as 'Air Commodore (Smith)'.

In Writing: Begin, 'Dear Air Commodore (Smith)'. Address the envelope 'Air Commodore (A. E. Smith)'.

Group Captain

In Speech and Writing: Address him as 'Group Captain (Smith)'. Address the envelope 'Group Captain (A. E. Smith)'.

Wing Commander

In Speech and Writing: Address him as 'Wing Commander (Smith)'. Address the envelope 'Wing Commander (A. E. Smith)'.

Squadron Leader

In Speech and Writing: Address him as 'Squadron Leader (Smith)'. Address the envelope 'Squadron Leader (A. E. Smith)'.

Flight Lieutenant

In Speech and Writing: Address him as 'Flight Lieutenant (Smith)'. Address the envelope 'Flight Lieutenant (A. E. Smith)'.

Below this rank Air Force titles are not used socially.

OTHER DIGNITARIES

Ambassador

In Speech: Formally he is addressed as 'Sir' or 'Your Excellency' and referred to as 'His Excellency'. Socially he is addressed as for his private rang, as 'Sir (John)' or 'Mr (Smith)'.

In Writing: The formal way to begin is 'Sir' or according to his rank; the social way is 'Dear Sir (John)' or 'Dear Mr (Smith)'. Address the envelope 'His Excellency, The British Ambassador', 'His Excellency, Sir (John Smith, KCMG)' or 'His Excellency (John Smith, CMG)'.

Ambassador's Wife

In Speech: Formally she is sometimes addressed as 'Your Excellency' and referred to as 'Her Excellency', but she is more often addressed as for her private rank, as 'Lady (Smith)' or 'Mrs (John Smith)'.

In Writing: Begin 'Madam', 'Dear Lady (Smith)' or 'Dear Mrs (Smith)'. Address the envelope 'Her Excellency Lady

---

EVEN IF THE FAMILY breadwinner earns only a modest salary it is possible for him to make substantial provision for his dependants if he should die. Whilst the old idea of providing a lump sum at death by means of an insurance policy saved much hardship it was rarely that a married man could afford to make provision for an *adequate lump sum*. The real problem was to replace his *income* should he die, sufficient to supplement his widow's state pension or widowed mother's allowance.

A lump sum provided by an insurance policy is not likely to go far when there are many years of rents and rates to pay, household repairs, school expenses, feeding and clothing growing children, and generally trying to maintain the standards to which the family are accustomed.

The Co-operative Insurance Society has the answer to this problem, known as the C.I.S. FAMILY PROTECTION PLAN. This provides a *guaranteed income* if the breadwinner should die before retirement age, together with substantial lump sum bene-fits. And if the unexpected and untimely does not happen, there is a large lump sum for him at retirement age, usually much larger than his total outlay under the Plan. The income benefits, according to the present practice of the Inland Revenue, are not subject to income tax, and they would not affect the widow's benefits under the National Insurance Scheme.

The C.I.S. FAMILY PROTEC-TION PLAN can be arranged to suit individual means and needs. It can provide the answer to your problem.

Write for details to-day.

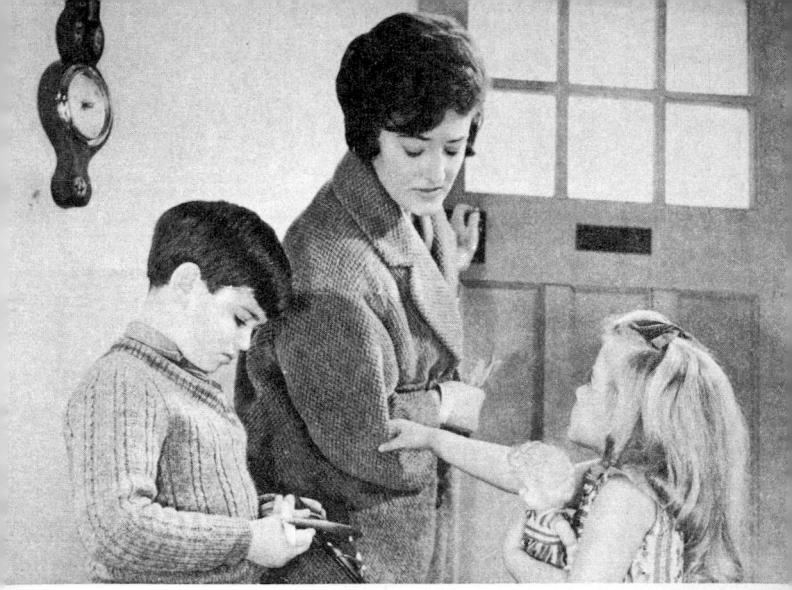

NEW PLAN PROTECTS DEPENDANTS
IF BREADWINNER DIES

POSTAGE WILL
BE PAID BY
CO-OPERATIVE
INSURANCE
SOCIETY LTD.

NO POSTAGE
STAMP
NECESSARY
IF POSTED IN
GT. BRITAIN
OR NORTHERN
IRELAND

BUSINESS REPLY SERVICE
Licence No. 9839

CO-OPERATIVE INSURANCE SOCIETY LTD.
109 CORPORATION STREET
MANCHESTER 4

(Smith)', 'Her Excellency Mrs (John Smith)' or simply
'Lady (Smith)' or 'Mrs (John Smith)'.

But when they are in this country an ambassador and his
wife are addressed as for their private rank only.

Lord Mayor

Letters are addressed 'The Rt. Hon. The Lord Mayor of
———' in the case of the Lord Mayors of London, York, Belfast,
Sydney (N.S. Wales), Melbourne (Victoria), Adelaide (S.
Australia), Perth (W. Australia), Brisbane (Queensland) and
Hobart (Tasmania). To other Lord Mayors the envelope is
addressed 'The Right Worshipful The Lord Mayor of ———'.
Address him formally both in speech and at the beginning of a
letter as 'My Lord'. Address him socially as for his private
rank.

Lord Mayor's Wife or Lady Mayoress

Address the envelope 'The Lady Mayoress'. Otherwise
address her as for her private rank.

Mayor

In Speech: On the bench a mayor is addressed as 'Your
Worship', otherwise as 'Mr Mayor' or, socially, according
to his or her private rank.

In Writing: Begin a formal letter 'Dear Mr Mayor', a social
letter 'Dear Mr (Smith)' or 'Dear Mrs (Smith)'. If the
mayor of a city, address the envelope 'The Right Worshipful The Mayor of ———'. If the mayor of a borough,
'The Worshipful the Mayor of ———'.

Mayor's Wife

On formal official occasions she is sometimes addressed as
'Mayoress'. Otherwise address her as for her private rank.

Justices of the Peace

When on the bench address them as 'Your Worship'. On a
letter addressed to them in their official capacity, add the
letters JP after their name. Otherwise address them as for their
private rank.

CHAPTER 7

TALKING

THIS IS not a book on grammar, but you can't discuss saying the right thing at the right time without mentioning it. The flagrant misuse of grammar is the worst solecism. You may win friends, but you are unlikely to influence people if, for instance, you are constantly using double negatives. The double negative as in, 'I can't come here no more', instead of the correct, 'I can't come here any more', brands the user as illiterate. Other common bad mistakes are: the use of 'me' instead of 'I' and vice versa, as in 'You and me think alike', and 'between you and I' instead of the correct, 'You and I think alike', and 'between you and me'; the use of the singular in place of the plural as in, 'We was going to the pictures', instead of the correct, 'We were going to the pictures'.

But curiously enough there are some grammatical errors to which society has given its blessing. They are not merely accepted, but anyone who used instead the grammatically correct form would be considered pedantic. The answer to 'Who's that?' is usually, 'It's me', instead of the grammatically correct, 'It's I'. Similarly it is incorrect, but usual to say, 'That's her', or 'That's him' and, 'Who did you give it to?'

ACCENTS

Some television personalities—and not only comedians—deliberately emphasize their parish pump accents, cashing in on the fact that, in a world that is becoming more and more uniform, any different way of speaking has a definite entertainment value.

But for ordinary men and women whose achievements and talents are not so outstanding as to give them a special claim on other people's indulgence, the sad truth is that certain accents can be an impediment both socially and in a career. Though Scottish (other than thick Glaswegian), Irish and Welsh accents are generally considered both charming and acceptable, any other local accent still carries the stigma of 'uneducated'. This is pure prejudice—some extremely well-educated people speak with a marked local accent—but there it is. One woman journalist got her first job on a small provincial newspaper, not because of her talents, but because the elderly woman proprietor said she spoke so nicely, meaning that she didn't speak with the local Berkshire accent.

The Cinderellas among accents, against which there is undoubtedly most prejudice, are the cockney and so-called 'genteel'. Anyone addressing an audience of BBC type speakers who starts by talking about 'putting the cart before the 'orse', has to have something very good indeed to say if he is to erase the initial bad impression made by that dropped 'H'.

The 'genteel' or 'refained' accent, by which I mean the pronunciation of 'nice' as 'naice', 'home' as 'haome', 'now' as 'naow', 'oh' as 'aoh', is not so much a disadvantage in most careers as it is socially, where it is considered the most damning of all the accents, probably because it is a bad imitation of the public school one. Since it is mainly confined to vowel sounds, however, this is not a difficult accent to cast.

Any accent always can be changed by anyone prepared to take the trouble, the most useful way of speaking to cultivate being the BBC type. Less exaggerated than the so-called 'Oxford accent' this is acceptable to people in all walks of life.

THE WORDS YOU USE

The French—aristocrats and bourgeois alike—say 'pardon', if they don't hear what you say. But if you say 'pardon' in English you risk being thought 'common' or 'genteel'. There is no good reason; it is purely a question of snobbery and fashion. The English upper classes, as a result of moving in the same isolated circles and going to the same schools, have developed their own peculiarities of speech and tend to look down on those who use alternative words and expressions. This prejudice is still extremely strong. Perhaps because they have lost most of their distinguishing characteristics—money, servants and large houses—they cling to this last bulwark between them and the rest. Whatever the ethics of it, if you mix with the English 'upper crust' you will get on a lot better if you speak as they do. On the left are the words and expressions they use, on the right those they consider 'common' or 'genteel'.

Sitting room, dining room or drawing room	Lounge (though you may talk about a lounge in a hotel)
Sofa	Couch (but a psychiatrist's couch is all right)
Lunch	Dinner (for the midday meal)
A 'drive' in his car	A 'ride' in his car
Riding	Horse-riding
'What?' 'What did you say?' or if you step on someone's toe, 'I'm sorry'	Pardon
Pudding	Afters
Lavatory or Loo (in a restaurant, you ask for the 'ladies cloakroom')	Toilet
Goodbye	Bye-bye
'Should I "change" (or "dress") for dinner?'	'Should I wear my dress suit?'
Thank you	Ta, Thanks ever so
'The tall woman over there.' But, 'The tall old lady over there'	'The tall lady over there'
'The tall man over there', also 'the tall old man'	'The tall gentleman over there'
Bathing suit	Bathing costume
Suit or coat-and-skirt	Costume
Scent	Perfume
My blue dress	My blue gown
Vegetables	Greens
False teeth	Dentures
Jam	Preserve
Please may I have . . .	Can I trouble you for . . .
Begin	Commence
Table napkin	Serviette
Make a remark	Pass a remark

Certain euphemisms are also considered genteel: He 'passed over' or 'passed away' for 'he died'; Uncle Edward's 'intoxicated' when Uncle Edward is plainly 'drunk'.

A word of warning though. Whenever a fashionable upper class word passes into general use it tends to be ejected from the upper class code and labelled 'common', as in the case of 'lady' or 'gentleman'.

So it is not impossible that in a few years' time the upper classes will be saying 'Pardon' and considering 'what' or 'what did you say' as 'distinctly common'!

FOREIGN WORDS

'Parliament having *d'oré la pillule* his Royal Highness is to swallow it . . .' wrote Sarah, Lady Lyttelton in a letter in 1809; and, 'We shall see the good Aumales tonight, who are staying with the Van de Weyers at New Lodge, which is *un vrai bijou* . . .' wrote Queen Victoria in 1860. In the last century it was fashionable to lard conversation and letters with as many French words and phrases as possible.

Now that going abroad is no longer confined to the upper classes, it is considered affected to use a foreign word where an English one will do and, in the case of words that have been absorbed into the English language, to give them their original pronunciation when there is an anglicized version. *Valet, Paris* and *cul de sac* for instance are pronounced as spelt. *Chauffeur* is pronounced *shofur*, *bouquet* as *bukay*, *champagne* as *shampain*, *billet doux* as *bilidoo*. These words have become part of our language and it would be quite wrong to treat them as though they were still French.

Where on the other hand there is no anglicized version—you can't for instance anglicize Champs Elysées—there is nothing for it but to get the pronunciation right or avoid the word altogether.

INTRODUCTIONS

There are two basic rules for introductions. (1) The man is always introduced to the woman, except when he is a much older and more important person. You would introduce a young girl to a bishop and not the other way round. And you would introduce the new typist to the director of the firm. (2) When both are of the same sex, the junior is always introduced to the senior person; a young girl is introduced to a middle-aged woman, a young man to an older man.

Except with royalty (see Chapter 13) no one uses the old-fashioned 'May I present . . .' More usual are: 'Mrs Bloggs, I don't think you've met Mr Smart,' 'Mrs Bloggs, do you know Mr Smart?' or 'Mrs Bloggs, this is Mr Smart.' In these forms the person whose name is said last is the person who is being introduced.

But introductions are becoming less and less formal. At parties today, your hostess is most likely to say simply, 'Mary Bloggs, Jane Smith', which has the advantage, when two people are of the same sex and age, of not making it clear whom you are introducing to whom.

Members of the Family

They are exceptions to the rule. Members of the family should be introduced to non-members of the family, unless there is a great discrepancy in age or status. A man taking his wife to his firm's annual party should introduce her to his colleagues, 'Mr Smith, I don't think you've met my wife; Mary, this is Mr Smith.' It is considered very bad form for a husband or wife to introduce each other as Mr or Mrs to people on the same or a higher social level.

If on the other hand a young girl brings her boy friend down to spend the weekend with her parents, she would say, 'Daddy and Mummy, this is John', introducing the boy friend to them since they are so much older.

When You Forget a Name

What should you do when as you are about to introduce someone their name goes clean out of your mind. Resourceful people have been known to say heartily, 'This is my very best friend. And here is Mary Smith.' And cowards to murmur, something unintelligible: 'Mary Smith', and vanish hastily to another part of the room leaving Mary Smith to find out his name for herself. But these methods rarely take anyone in. The best policy is to own up: 'It's idiotic of me, but I've forgotten your name.' He is unlikely to be offended, as this situation will almost certainly have happened to him sometime, too.

Alternatively, you can hum and haw several times before introducing the person whose name you've forgotten. Usually they will say their own name out of sheer self-preservation!

At Parties

The best hostesses are those who don't simply say, 'Mary Smith, John Jones', and leave them wondering how on earth to start a conversation, but give some sort of cue. It doesn't really matter how slight. 'Mary's mad about tennis, too', or, 'John's a lepidopterist', may not lead the way to sparkling witticisms but it does at least give Mary and John something a little less banal to open with than the stock: 'What do you do?'

And if Mary doesn't know what lepidopterist means she can always start the conversation by asking him.

In the Street and in Restaurants

Suppose when you're with a friend in a restaurant or in the street you see someone you know? If you greet the person and pass on, it's unnecessary to do any introducing. But if you stop for a long chat, it's obviously bad manners to leave your friend out of the picture and you must introduce him or her.

GREETINGS

The correct thing to say when you meet someone for the first time is, 'How do you do'. This is just a more formal way of saying 'Hallo' and the correct reply is also 'How do you do', not 'Very well, thank you' or 'My feet are killing me'. 'How are you' is usually just as meaningless, but it does seem to require some kind of answer. Most people settle for 'Very well, thank you' or 'fine, thank you'.

What you are never supposed to say is 'Pleased to meet you'. For some unknown reason this is considered 'common'.

GOODBYES

Sticklers for good form maintain that the correct thing to say is simply 'Goodbye' and leave it at that; on no account should you say, 'Pleased to have met you'. But there are occasions, when you have met someone or had them to stay for the first time, for instance, when just 'Goodbye' seems a little cold. 'It's been so nice meeting you', 'I hope we meet again', 'You must come again', are all possible.

SHAKING HANDS

When to shake hands? Always if someone offers to shake hands with you. Otherwise there is no rule. As a whole, unlike other nationalities, we tend not to shake hands at parties—a boon to women who need three hands anyway, one for their handbag, one for their drink and one for their cigarette. But it's no longer true to say that the upper classes tend to shake hands less than the lower. These days people do whatever seems the friendliest or most courteous thing at the time.

SMALL TALK

The woman who believes in remaining silent unless she has something worthwhile to say is a social wet blanket. Small talk is essentially light-hearted and superficial and it is much more important to keep the ball in the air than to produce a memorable remark. Never answer a question with a simple 'No' or 'Yes' or 'I don't agree', always contribute something of your own that can serve as a cue to the next speaker.

The topics to bring up at a social gathering are any common denominators. Servants used to be a very usual gambit. It has been said that the servants used to be in the servants' hall discussing the gentry and the gentry in the drawing room discussing the servants. The disappearance of servants from the houses of all but the very rich has made them no longer a useful subject. But what small talk has lost on the swings with servants, it has gained on the roundabouts with television and washing machines. Everyone has something to say about them. Children, clothes, cooking and royalty are sure-fire topics among any group of women. Cooking and washing-up have even become possible with some men. Two judges at the Garrick Club in London have been overheard discussing the best way to wash up the china.

Another sure-fire topic is anything in the news—Wimbledon if it's Wimbledon week, the current strike and that case in the law courts; good small talkers are avid newspaper readers. Books, films and plays are useful too, but only among people likely to know about them.

Of course, there are some talkers so entertaining that they

can afford to hold forth on a subject about which the rest of the party know nothing. But, if no one else is allowed to get a word in, they have got to be really entertaining or they will be considered bores. Most of us would selfishly rather sparkle ourselves than watch other people sparkling—which is why a shy person can get by very well if she sticks to asking other people's opinions and listening appreciatively to the answers.

SUBJECTS TO AVOID

Politics, religion and sex, it used to be said, were three topics that should never be brought up at a social gathering. This seems old-fashioned to us today, but the fact behind the Victorian tabu remains; these subjects are still those most likely to raise tempers and provoke furious argument.

It is not bad manners today to talk about politics at a dinner party, but it is bad manners if it sparks off a violent row. And if you're not absolutely sure when you introduce one of these subjects that you won't be treading on any toes it's much better to leave it alone.

If you know that the other guests share your religious belief you can safely criticize other denominations. If you know everyone else in the room is left-wing, you can safely criticize right-wing politics. But if you don't know this, beware. Many friendships came adrift as the result of arguments on Suez which years later have not fully recovered.

Another Victorian tabu was that 'nice people don't discuss other people'. This is now completely outdated. One of the easiest ways to start a conversation is to talk about a mutual friend. Though it is obviously tactful to keep your comments complimentary, at least until you know what sort of relationship exists between the person you are talking about and the person you are talking to. It's all too easy to mention 'the girl in the terrible dress over there' only to find she's his wife.

Gossip is one of the mainstays of small talk and one usually finds those who deride it most indulge in it just as much as everyone else. Everyone can't talk intelligently on films and books, but they can express interest in the fact that John Smith is getting married to that pretty model.

Gossip need not necessarily be malicious, though the sad

truth is that it is much easier to be amusing about people's faults than their virtues. But ethics apart, anyone who goes in for malicious gossip must be prepared for it to get back to its subject as it almost invariably does.

MONEY

The pendulum of fashion has swung. It used to be considered bad form to mention it. Now this attitude is considered 'genteel' and the more 'upper class' the group of people, the more frequently does the subject crop up, the iniquity of income tax, the cost of houses, flats, food. Money is one of the common denominators and a useful social gambit. Nobody has enough of it and everyone has something to say about it. Since so many of the old families who used to have money no longer have it, it has become almost fashionable to be hard up. Women are much more likely to boast that they got a dress in a sale for three pounds than that they paid forty.

Very few people however come out with exact figures of income and earnings. And it is still tactless to ask anyone but an intimate friend a direct question: 'How much did that dress cost?'; 'What did you pay for your house?' or, 'How much do you earn?'

SHOP

This is another Victorian tabu that is no longer valid. Whether you should talk shop or not today depends not on etiquette but how the person you are talking to feels about it. Many people enjoy talking about their jobs and are more interesting on this subject than on any other. Inviting them to talk shop may give them an opportunity to shine which they would not otherwise get.

But people who don't particularly enjoy their jobs or who work very hard at them may prefer to get right away in their leisure hours. Doctors and psychologists for instance rarely want to talk about medicine or psychology at a party. Again people who do some highly specialized work may not want to discuss it with those who know nothing about it. Poets often object to being talked to about their poetry, especially by anyone who is not a poet himself yet sets up as a critic. As Edith

Sitwell said, 'I don't like talking to people who try to teach me my job—after all I don't try to teach plumbers their job.'

One time when it *is* bad manners to talk shop is in a small gathering of people most but not all of whom belong to the same profession, since those who don't will be left out of the conversation.

Tactless Questions

People are less secretive about their ages than they were. Victorian mothers often disguised their ages even from their own daughters. But it is still not tactful to ask anyone over the age of thirty, 'How old are you?' And if you do ask you are five out of ten times not going to get a truthful answer. Pretending to be twenty-nine may not make one a day less than thirty-five, but many women still persist in the myth that by ignoring time they can cheat it. Even when they are plainly elderly some women still go on lying about their age. And not only women. Men often knock off a year or two for the sake of their careers or simply an almost feminine vanity.

'When are you two going to get married?' This again is not a tactful question. But it's frequently asked all the same. The chances are either that he hasn't asked her or that they have been arguing hotly on the subject for some time. A useful reply is a light-hearted, 'We're just good friends', which is so hackneyed that it can mean anything.

Compliments

The English woman's typical answer to the compliment 'what a pretty dress!' is, 'Oh do you think so? I'm not sure about the colour', or 'Actually if you look closely the seams aren't straight'. This is where the Americans show much better manners than we. They say, 'Thank you', thus accepting the compliment gracefully instead of under the cloak of modesty virtually flinging it back in the complimenter's face. Perhaps it is because English women are so bad at receiving compliments that English men are famous for being bad at paying them. . . .

APOLOGIES

Apologies are embarrassing to both parties and in any case can't undo the damage. The best policy is to say you're sorry once as though you really meant it and leave it at that. The person apologized to is supposed to say, 'It doesn't matter', sounding as sincere as she can even though her precious Sèvres vase lies shattered at her feet.

INTERRUPTING

This is a very common fault, but it is bad manners. Good manners require you to let the other person finish regardless of the fact that by that time the funny story you were about to tell may no longer be appropriate.

CONTRADICTING

There are comparatively tactful ways of pointing out that someone's under a mistaken impression, but a flat contradiction is not among them. A sentence beginning, 'That's wrong', or, 'That's not true', may come to exactly the same thing as a sentence that begins, 'Don't you think that', but the former is a great deal ruder and more likely to lead to raised tempers.

SWEARING

If your husband said 'damn' fifty years ago, you told your friends about it in a shocked whisper. 'Dash' and 'bother' were the strongest expletives a lady would allow herself. Nowadays there are few people who have not in moments of stress said worse than 'damn'. Constant use takes the shockingness out of swearwords, the original meaning is forgotten and they become just a noise that expresses our feelings when we are annoyed.

But since one of the criterions of good manners is to avoid offending other people's susceptibilities, before you give voice to your favourite expletive, it is advisable to consider whether it will be as meaningless to the people you are with as it is to you. Very especially to be avoided are any swearwords that might offend other people's religion. And incidentally the men who are themselves heavy swearers are often just as horrified as Aunt Emma to hear women follow suit.

D. H. Lawrence is said to have been profoundly shocked

when Aldous Huxley's Belgian wife, who typed out the manuscript of *Lady Chatterley's Lover*, used some of its four-letter words.

SLANG

There is nothing wrong with using slang. Many of the words and phrases are extremely efficient and colourful and the language would be the poorer without them. He went down the street *like greased lightning*; she looked at me *as though I was something the cat had brought in*; he's *pushing up the daisies*. Many of the words and phrases that are slang today are accepted as standard English tomorrow.

But some slang peculiar to a certain set it is bad lifemanship to use outside that set. *Harry champers* for champagne, a *splendid* girl, a *fabulous* man, *utter bliss*, the *chic* thing to do, *one* just doesn't does *one*, *shekels* for money, and *long time no see*, sound both ridiculous and affected to people not used to expressing themselves in this way.

AMERICANISMS

Fix up, meaning organize, *standpoint*, meaning point of view, and *back number*, meaning antiquated, are three Americanisms deplored by Fowler in 1930. Try as the guardians of the English language do to keep Americanisms out they continue to find their way into our vocabulary. In a few years' time we shall probably all be using *I guess* instead of *I suppose*; *maybe* instead of *perhaps*; *sure* instead of *yes certainly*; the pronunciation *skedule* for *schedule* and *formidable* instead of *fórmidable*.

The leadership of the world has passed out of English into American hands and it is American and not English that most foreigners learn today. But meanwhile we cling jealously to our own language and accuse any English person who uses Americanisms of speaking bad English.

WHAT TO SAY IF YOU ARE ASKED TO . . .
. . . *Open a Bazaar or Fête*

What is said on these occasions runs very much to a pattern. Here are some signposts. Say what a good cause the bazaar is in aid of and, if you like, say something about the cause and what the target of the bazaar is. You can mention the weather —if it's fine, you can say you hope this will inspire people to spend lavishly. If it's raining, you can say that you hope people will spend lavishly nevertheless. Thank the organizers for all their work and if anyone has been particularly active mention them by name. Mention any particular attractions the bazaar has. End by saying, 'I declare this bazaar open.'

Suggestion for an opening: 'Ladies and gentlemen. It was a very pleasant surprise to me when I was asked to come and open this bazaar. I have long been interested in (name of charity) . . .'

Shy people can console themselves with the thought that the shorter the opening address, the more popular it usually is.

. . . Present Prizes

It is unnecessary to say more than a very few introductory words along these lines: 'I am sure we all feel delighted at the great success of . . .', or, 'It gives me great pleasure to hand the prizes to the successful competitors'; if the competition is a children's obstacle race, you could add, 'who certainly fully deserve them!' If the winner is well known to everyone present you could say something about him or her or, if you like, something about the competition or something about the qualities needed for success.

. . . Introduce a Speaker

Begin with some welcoming phrase such as: 'We are very pleased to have Lady Smith with us today and flattered that, in spite of her numerous engagements, she has found time to fit us in.' Give reasons why Lady Smith is so well qualified to speak on the subject of her forthcoming address. Finish by saying, 'Ladies and Gentlemen, Lady Smith.'

. . . Propose a Vote of Thanks

This can be very brief, simply: 'I have much pleasure in proposing a vote of thanks to Lady Smith for her most interesting talk.' If you like you can add some comment on any aspect of the talk you found particularly interesting.

The formal way is to begin: 'Ladies and Gentlemen' unless distinguished people with titles are present in which case these are mentioned first. If the Queen were present you would begin, 'Your Majesty, Ladies and Gentlemen'; if a member of the royal family, 'Your Royal Highness, Ladies and Gentlemen'; if a Duke, Duchess or Archbishop, 'Your Grace, Ladies and Gentlemen'; if a Peer, 'My Lord, Ladies and Gentlemen'; if a Lord Mayor, 'My Lord Mayor, Ladies and Gentlemen'.

Where only women are present the form is simply, 'Ladies'. Where just one man is present the usual form is, 'Mr Smith, Ladies . . .'

TOASTS

Toasts after lunch or dinner are proposed when coffee has been served, by the chairman if there is one, the senior man present or anyone else specially qualified. If the dinner is in honour of a special guest something complimentary should be said about him or her, and the particular reason for celebrating should be mentioned. A brief re-cap of the guest's achievements or services may be appropriate, also humorous recollections and allusions likely to appeal to the listeners. The toast is proposed at the end of the speech. The proposer holds up his glass and says simply, 'Mr Blank'.

Everyone present except the person or people toasted then stands up to drink his or their health.

What do you do if there is nothing left in your glass? Simply tilt it and pretend; it's all symbolic anyway.

A toast normally calls for a reply in a similar vein, though the opportunity may be taken to add or emphasize some personal views on a serious subject.

At a formal dinner, the person replying to the toast would not propose another toast. But on a less formal occasion people please themselves; at a wedding reception, for instance, the bridegroom replies to the toast to the bride and groom and usually ends by proposing a toast to the bridesmaids.

Here are some useful stock phrases: 'It is my pleasant duty to propose the toast to ——'; 'It is my privilege to propose the

toast to ——'; 'I have been honoured by being asked to propose the toast to ——'; 'I know you will all want to join with
me in drinking to the success of ——'.

Tip for anyone faced with making a speech for the first
time: keep it short. The following reply to a Toast to the
Guests coming at the end of a succession of long speeches went
down extremely well:

'Though I may not look as young as I am this is the first
time I have been asked to make a speech. I know there is one
quality in maiden speakers that always wins the applause of
the audience, and that is brevity. So I will simply say on
behalf of the guests, thank you, thank you very much.'

A Toast to the Ladies

Unless one of them has been asked beforehand it is not
generally considered necessary for them to reply. Though, of
course, one of the ladies can retaliate by proposing a toast to
the gentlemen!

Christmas Toasts

Many families who have an annual get-together at Christmas like to round off the meal with toasts usually proposed by
the senior member of the family; a toast to the Queen, a toast
to Absent Friends, and a toast to the hostess. These toasts are
not usually preceded by speeches.

Twenty-first Birthday Party

The old friend of the family who proposes the toast says
something complimentary about the boy or girl, refers to the
importance of the age of twenty-one and finishes by wishing
him or her every happiness and success. The hero or heroine
of the hour need only reply very briefly saying: 'Thank you for
all the nice things you have said about me and thank you all
for your good wishes.' Though they can if they like, of course,
make a longer speech.

CHAPTER 8

WRITING

'THERE IS no greater opportunity to show good taste—or bad —than in the type of notepaper you use' states a 1920s etiquette book. While it would be a gross exaggeration to say that today, certain tabus about personal writing paper persist. Any colours other than white, cream, grey or blue are considered bad taste and the same applies to rough or scalloped edges and coloured borders. Plainness is considered synonymous with good taste. But there is no longer any tabu about the shape or size of envelope or paper. The ridiculous notion that an envelope with a pointed flap was in better taste than a rounded or straight-across flap is mercifully outdated. The fact that single sheets of writing paper are more often used than the once fashionable double sheets has nothing to do with etiquette; they are simply more economical.

HEADED WRITING PAPER

Though printed headings are usual for business, it is still not considered 'done' to have your address and telephone number printed on your personal writing paper. It is better to write it by hand or type it. Best and smartest of all is to have it engraved. The usual colours for engraved headings are blue on blue paper, red on grey paper, black or blue on white or cream paper. It should be set either in the centre of the top of the page or, indented, in the right-hand top corner, the lettering absolutely plain, all capitals being more usual than capitals and small letters, *eg:*

STICKLEBACK MANSIONS   28 ABERCROMBY GARDENS
BELTON SQUARE   HELMFORTH ROAD
LONDON SW3   TEL. 1945   FOLKESTONE
FLAXMAN 92256

When the address is in the right-hand corner, the telephone number is sometimes put across the opposite left-hand corner.

For brief notes some people use a small sheet of writing paper with the address and telephone number engraved along the width, *eg:*

19 PUTLEY STREET, LONDON, SW3   Sloane 12345

LAYOUT FOR A PERSONAL LETTER

The first essential is that it should be as pleasant as possible to look at—a short letter should be centred in the middle of the page, never bunched up at the top with an ugly waste of space beneath the signature.

When the address is hand-written or typed the date is usually, but not always, put directly underneath. When the address is engraved, people fit the date in where they can.

In formal letters, people give the year as well as the day and the month, 27th June, 1961 or 27/6/61; in letters to close friends, people often simply scrawl Saturday or Wednesday. The 'Yours sincerely' etc should begin underneath the last sentence of the letter, in the centre of the page.

LAYOUT FOR A BUSINESS LETTER

The name and address of the person you are writing to should be put on the left-hand side of the page either below your own address or below your signature. This is the conventional way to set out any letter on business whether typed or hand-written:

19 Putley Street,
London SW3
January 5th, 1962

The Manager,
Plum and Bodsworth Ltd.,
Appleton Square,
London, SW5

Dear Sir,

Or:

Yours faithfully,

The Manager,
Plum and Bodsworth Ltd.,
Appleton Square,
London, SW5

Typed Private Letters

Many professional people find it more convenient to type their private letters than to write them by hand. But there is a rather cold, impersonal feeling about a typewritten letter—especially if the writer has a secretary and there is a chance he may simply have dictated it. One way to get over this impersonal feeling is to hand-write the 'Dear Mary' or 'Dear Mr Smith' and also the 'Love from' or 'Yours sincerely' and add a few words by hand at the bottom of the letter.

But letters of condolence being of a very personal nature should be hand-written throughout.

Addressing the Envelope

Name and address should be roughly in the centre of the envelope. When they are typed they may either be indented or put one underneath the other:

> Mrs A. B. Smith,
> The Grange,
> Little Newington,
> Hertfordshire.

When they are hand-written it is usual to indent:

> Mrs A. B. Smith,
> The Grange,
> Little Newington,
> Hertfordshire.

It is not considered 'done' to write the address or any part of the address in quotation marks, *eg* 'The Grange'.

Esquire

The days when 'Esq.' was used only after the name of a member of the upper classes and everyone else was addressed as 'Mr' are no longer with us. Though people lucky enough to employ men servants still do not address them as 'Esq.', the safe general rule for anyone else who doesn't want to risk giving offence is to address all untitled men as 'Esq.' regardless of status or family tree.

'John Smith, Esq.', is the usual form when you know his christian name, if you don't you give him his initials, 'J. S. Smith, Esq.'.

What should you do when you don't know his initials? Since some people, for some unknown reason consider '— Smith, Esq.' bad manners, the only solution is to guess.

Married Women

The old-fashioned rule that the senior married woman of the family was addressed as 'Mrs Smith', the others as 'Mrs (husband's christian name or initials) Smith' is now rarely observed, since it entails knowing all about the family. 'Mrs (husband's christian name or initials) Smith' is the usual style of address for all married women today.

Widows

They are addressed in exactly the same way as when their husbands were alive. (For widows of peers and baronets see Chapter 6.)

Divorced Women who have not Re-married

Address them by their own christian name or initials and their ex-husband's surname, 'Mrs Mary Smith'.

Professional Married Women

Letters sent to them in their professional capacity are usually addressed 'Mrs (her own christian name and husband's surname)'.

Addressing Husband and Wife together

Write: 'Mr and Mrs (husband's christian name or initials) Smith'.

Unmarried Women

Formerly, the rule was that the senior unmarried woman in the family was known simply as 'Miss Smith', the others as 'Miss Mary (or initials) Smith'. This is rarely observed today, the usual style of address for all unmarried women being 'Miss Mary (or initials) Smith'.

Two sisters together are addressed as The Misses Smith.

Children

Girls are addressed as 'Miss Mary (or initials) Smith', boys simply as 'John (or initials) Smith'.

Care Of

It is considered good manners when you write to a friend staying in someone else's house to include the name of her hostess on the envelope:

Miss Mary Smith,
c/o Mrs John Brown,
The Grange.

Messrs. and Ltd.

It is incorrect to use them both on the same envelope. A limited company should be addressed as, 'Jones and Brown Ltd.' 'Messrs.' should be used only when addressing a partnership, 'Messrs. Jones and Brown'. But when the name of a partnership is preceded by 'the' or a title, 'Messrs.' is not used, *eg*, 'The British Blanket Company', 'Sir John Smith & Co.' If you don't know whether a firm is a partnership or a limited company, it is perfectly correct to write the name of the firm, 'Jones and Brown', and leave it at that.

BEGINNINGS

'My Dear' once used in preference to 'Dear' to friends and social acquaintances is going out of fashion. Most people today begin plain 'Dear' both to lifelong friends and to the plumber. Business letters usually begin 'Dear Sir' or 'Dear Madam', if you haven't met the person you are writing to, even though you know their name and use it in the address. 'Dear Sir or Madam' is the form when you don't know the sex of the person you are writing to, 'Dear Sirs' when you are writing to a corporate group of people, such as a shop, rather than an individual.

A new way of beginning used a great deal in BBC circles is, 'Dear Mary Smith', less formal than 'Dear Miss Smith', not quite so informal as 'Dear Mary'.

ENDINGS

Those most generally in use today are 'Love from' to intimate friends and relations, 'Yours' to people you address by their christian name but don't know well enough to send your love to, 'Yours sincerely' to anyone you address by their surname, whether social or business acquaintances, 'Yours faithfully' or 'Yours truly', when the letter begins 'Dear Sir etc'. A cordial note is often lent to 'Yours sincerely' by the addition of 'Best wishes' or 'Kind regards'.

At the end of a typed business letter it is usual to type your name and, if you are writing on behalf of a firm, your position, under your signature, 'Mary Smith, Features Editor'. If your letter is hand-written and the person you are writing to doesn't know whether you are Miss or Mrs, it is usual to add it in brackets beside your signature, 'Mary Smith (Mrs)'.

LETTERS AFTER PEOPLE'S NAMES

These fall into three categories: Crown Honours—that is any orders or decorations whether for civil or active service, conferred by the Queen; membership of learned societies, etc; letters indicating academic distinctions, professional or official status. Letters after a name should be written in the order given in the reference books.

Crown Honours

These should be added on an envelope unless you know that the person you are writing to prefers not to use them. But if someone has a whole string of letters after his name, the letters standing for the most distinguished honour or honours only need be used. Though some people with minor honours only, such as an MBE, prefer not to use them, unless you know this it is courteous to add them. But if a man has a minor crown honour and also a relatively much greater distinction in another field, you might leave out the crown honour. When writing to a man with an MBE who is also a Fellow of the Royal Society, for instance, you might give him his FRS and leave out the MBE.

Letters standing for membership of learned societies, etc, are added usually only if they imply special distinction. (For letters standing for professional qualifications see paragraph below.) You would add FRS (Fellow of the Royal Society), FBA (Fellow of the British Academy), FSA (Fellow of the Society of Antiquaries of London), RA (Royal Academician), ARA (Associate of the Royal Academy) for instance, but not FRHistS (Fellow of the Royal Historical Society) or FRGS (Fellow of the Royal Geographical Society).

Letters indicating Professional or Official Status and Academic Distinctions

QC (Queen's Counsel) and MP should always be added. PC (Privy Councillor) is not used when addressing anyone below the rank of Marquess, The Right Hon. being used as a prefix instead. Other letters indicating professional or official status are not generally used in private correspondence, but they should be used when writing to their owners in an official or professional capacity. Letters denoting Masters' or Bachelors' degrees, MA, BA, BSc, etc, are rarely used except when writing to someone in the teaching profession.

CONTENT OF LETTERS

Gone is the idea that a letter should be written in a careful prose style that bears little relation to speech. True, most people are more careful of their grammar when they are writing than when they are talking, but otherwise the fashion is for letters to be as colloquial as possible. 'Can't', 'shan't' and 'won't' are now written as well as spoken and it is no longer considered impolite to write '&' for 'and'.

All this however has not altered the fact that certain types of letters are still tricky for those faced with writing them for the first time.

THANK-YOU LETTERS

It's time-saving as well as good manners to write them as promptly as possible. Two brief paragraphs are perfectly acceptable if you write immediately. But if you put it off for several weeks, you should write a longer letter.

Bread-and-Butter

After spending a night in someone else's house, however sincerely you may have said thank you when you left, you should still write a thank-you letter. One sentence of thanks followed by a description of your life and loves since is not generally considered enough except to intimate friends. The form is to say why you enjoyed yourself and to mention any aspect of your stay which gave you particular pleasure.

Here is a letter from a girl who had been to stay with her boy friend's parents:

Dear Mrs Smith,

      I did so enjoy my weekend with you. It was a real treat for me to get out of London into the country—such a lovely part of the country, too—and a wonderful rest from my usual weekend chores. The Point to Point was great fun —it is the first time I have been to one.

      The roads were surprisingly clear on the way back. Tom and I got to London in under an hour.

      Again, thank you so very much.

Yours sincerely,
Mary Brown.

Thank You for a Present

Like bread-and-butter letters the best thank-you-for-a-present letters contain more than one sentence of thanks. The form is to say why the present is just what you wanted, 'though we have received seven clocks and three toast racks, until your present arrived we had not got a single saucepan', or to give some sort of picture of it in use, 'the vase looks lovely against the grey walls of our sitting room and cheers us up whenever we look at it'.

LETTERS OF CONDOLENCE

It is impossible to lay down any hard and fast formula for a letter of condolence. Obviously your own personal feelings and the character of the person you are writing to must be your guide. But most of us are so unaccustomed to expressing our deep feelings on paper that the following tips may help.

The purpose of a letter of condolence is to console the living and the way to do that is not to harp on the tragic aspects of death but if possible to find the silver lining in the cloud. 'I am sure that is the way he would have liked to have died' is far more consoling than 'What a terrible way to end!' If you can refer to any happy memories of the dead man or woman, the full and happy life they led, or the good that they did, that will help, too.

The most difficult letter of condolence to write is to someone you don't know very well. Here is an example:

> I felt I had to write and tell you how sorry I was to read of your mother's death. We both have very happy memories of our visits to 10 Godfrey Street. What a wonderful old lady she was, so up-to-date and interested in everything. I only hope I shall get as much out of life as she did if ever I reach her age.
>
> I know there is no real consolation, but please believe me that you have all our sympathy.

LETTERS OF CONGRATULATION

Congratulations on an appointment, an honour or passing an examination run very much to a pattern. You begin by saying how delighted you are to hear the news, go on to say how well he or she has deserved whatever it is and why.

BUSINESS LETTERS

Except in a few long-established firms which cling to the old forms, business letters no longer have a language all their own. Commercialese like, *Awaiting the favour of your reply, I oblige, Thanking you in anticipation* and *Re yours of the 20th ult.* has gone out of fashion. Most business letters today begin, *Thank you for your letter of September 20th*, or, *In answer to your letter of September 20th.*

People who use long-winded phrases like *In order to obviate time wastage on either part* instead of simply *So as not to waste time*, impress nobody but themselves. The way to write a good business letter is to state your case as simply and clearly as possible, *eg:*

Letter to a Bank

Dear Sir,

Please will you send me a new cheque book containing 24 cheques.

Yours faithfully,

Mary Smith (Mrs).

Letter of Complaint to a Shop

Dear Sirs,

On Monday June 20th, I bought a navy blue and white striped skirt price £5 5s at your shop. The label said drip-dry. I followed the washing instructions carefully, but in spite of this the navy blue has run into the white and the skirt is now completely unwearable.

I would be grateful if you would give me a credit for the cost of the skirt or return my money.

Yours faithfully,

INVITATION CARDS

The whole business of invitation cards is fraught with tricky little points of etiquette that, trivial or old-fashioned as they may seem, are still very widely observed. And, after all, sending cards instead of writing to or ringing up your friends is a formal thing to do, and there are right and wrong ways of doing it.

Which kind of card out of the large and confusing variety in the shops in every sort of lettering on every sort of paper should you choose? By no means all of them are correct. Deckled edges, cocktail glasses, wedding bells, horseshoes and other jolly or sentimental decorations, however suitable to the occasion, are considered to be in bad taste. As with writing paper, the rule is the plainer, the better. Lettering should always be black, never silver or coloured, on plain, good-quality paper.

The etiquette of invitation cards has changed very little during the last few years. But one concession has been made to modern budgets. Though it's grander to have your cards engraved, it is no longer a social solecism to have them printed. Brides' mothers faced with the enormous expense of even the simplest wedding have gone on strike. Invitations to all but the most fashionable society weddings today are printed, as are invitations to many cocktail parties. But cards are still engraved for very formal occasions such as coming-out dances and elaborate dinner parties.

Lettering on an engraved card should be copperplate, letterpress script on a printed card.

Little Points

Here are some of the details that distinguish the most correct cards. The day and the month should be given, but never the year, Saturday June 3rd, never Saturday June 3rd, 1961. For some reason, o'clock is considered superior to am or pm. There is a school of thought which claims that the RSVP should always be on the right hand side, but some of the cards sent out by the 'best' people have the RSVP on the left.

Envelopes

The strictly correct thing to do, when sending an invitation to a married couple, is to write the wife's name only on the envelope. But young people today when inviting friends of their own age usually disregard that rule and address the envelope to both.

Formally the envelope should be sealed, but this again is a rule that few young people today observe, since postage is expensive.

Guests' Names on Cards

A married couple are addressed as, *Mr and Mrs John Smith*. If you want to invite the children as well, you add, *and family*. A single man is addressed as, *Mr John Smith*. If you are inviting two sisters, Mary and Belinda Smith, *Miss Belinda Smith* is written under *Miss Mary Smith*.

If you were inviting a Duke and Duchess you would write *The Duke and Duchess of (Hampstead)*. All other peers and peeresses are addressed as *Lord and Lady (Hampstead)*.

E   113

Baronets and knights and their wives are addressed as *Sir John and Lady (Smith)*. When a woman with a title in her own right is married to a commoner, you address them as *Mr John and Lady (Mary Smith)*.

The prefix Hon. or letters after names are never used on invitation cards.

In the case of a married couple where the husband has a clerical or service rank, the form is *The Bishop of (Barchester) and Mrs (A. E. Smith)*, *Admiral and Mrs (A. E. Smith)*. A doctor and his wife are addressed as *Dr and Mrs (A. E. Smith)*, a vicar or rector and his wife as *The Rev. and Mrs (A. E. Smith)*.

When a man has both a service rank and a title, usually only the title is used on the card. Admiral Sir John and Lady Smith would be addressed simply as, *Sir John and Lady Smith*.

Wedding Invitation

This should be a folded white sheet of paper with the information engraved or printed on the outside and the guests' names hand-written in the top left-hand corner. The bridegroom's full name is given but only the bride's christian names. The rest of the information should be given as briefly as possible as in the example below.

Sir Anthony and Lady Douglas

Mr and Mrs David Hedges
request the pleasure of your company
at the marriage of their daughter
Mary Rose
to
Mr John Maxwell Harding
at St Margaret's, Westminster
on Saturday, June 3rd
at 2 o'clock
and afterwards at
the Hyde Park Hotel

The Old Grange,
Grampton,
Hertfordshire.

RSVP

It is becoming more and more usual for divorced parents to join forces for a daughter's wedding, in which case the invitation begins:

Mr James Brown

and

Mrs Paul Armstrong

request the pleasure of your company

When the bride's mother is on her own the invitation begins:

Mrs Peter Danvers

requests the pleasure of your company

at the marriage of her daughter

If the host and hostess are the bride's uncle and aunt, the invitation begins:

Lieut-Colonel and Mrs Simon Brownlow

request the pleasure of your company

at the marriage of their niece

When for some reason the guests are to be invited to a reception only—perhaps the church is too small to hold everyone or the wedding is in a register office—the invitation begins:

Mr and Mrs Jeremy Johns

request the pleasure of your company

at a reception

after the marriage of their daughter

The best person to advise you on layout if you want any variation on the traditional wording is your printer.

Cocktail Party Invitations

The correct cocktail party invitation when it is filled in reads like this:

Mr & Mrs John Smith

Mrs Peter Potts

at Home

Thursday May 11th

Cocktails

6 o'clock

23 Elm Square,
    SW1.   **RSVP**

On the grandest cards Mrs Peter Potts, at Home, RSVP and the address are engraved and the other details handwritten in. But equally acceptable and less expensive are cards that have the at Home, Cocktails and RSVP only engraved or printed. Before they are filled in, these cards look like this:

....

at Home

....

RSVP

Cocktails

Formally, when a married couple give a party—except a lunch, dinner or wedding reception—only the name of the hostess should appear on the invitation card. But for informal parties, where everyone is on christian name terms, many young people today dispense with this tradition and send out cards that read like this:

John & Mary Smith

Peter and Jane Green
at Home
Friday May 12th

Cocktails

23 Elm Square,   6 o'clock
SW1.   RSVP

Similarly young unmarried men and girls sending invitations usually call themselves simply, 'Mary Smith' or 'John Smith', without a Mr or Miss, addressing older guests only as 'Mr and Mrs John Smith', people of their own age as plain 'John Smith' or 'Mary Smith'.

Dinner Party Invitations

An 'At Home' card may be used with the word Dinner in place of Cocktails. Or an engraved or printed card may be sent which, when filled in, reads like this:

Mr and Mrs John Smith
request the pleasure of
Mr and Mrs Gerald Brown's
company at dinner on Tuesday
January 3rd at 7 o'clock

Milton Hall,
   Hampworth,
      Buckinghamshire.
                                  RSVP

On a specially engraved card the names of the guests, the day, the date and the time only are written in by hand. On the ready-printed cards that can be bought in the shops the names of host and hostess and the address are also written in.

Twenty-first Birthday Invitation

The form for a twenty-first birthday invitation is:

Mr and Mrs John Smith
request the pleasure of the company of
....
to celebrate the Coming of Age
of their daughter
Mary Rose
at the Park Lane Hotel, London W1,
on Saturday, March 25th

                     Dancing 9 o'clock

14 Elm Square,
   SW1.
                                  RSVP

Bridge or Bottle Parties

Use an ordinary 'At Home' card with 'Bridge' or 'Bottle Party' hand-written in where cocktails usually goes. Some people specify the type of bottle in brackets.

Dance Invitations

For an informal dance an ordinary 'At Home' card can be used, filled in in exactly the same way as for a cocktail party except that 'Dancing' and the time the dancing is to start is put where the word cocktails usually goes. For a formal dance all the information is engraved and the card is larger.

When the dance is not being given at the address guests are to RSVP to, the card reads like this:

Miss Carolyn Poultney Smith
Lady Brown
at Home
Wednesday, May 20th
23 Knightsbridge

RSVP
26 Elmbond Square   Dancing 10 o'clock
SW3.

When the dance is shared the card reads like this:

Lady Brown
Mrs John Smith
at Home
Wednesday, May 30th
23 Knightsbridge

RSVP
26 Elmbond Square,   Dancing 10 o'clock
SW3.

For a coming-out dance, invitations may be as above or they may include the girls' names, *eg*:

Lady Brown and Mrs John Smith
at Home
for
Mary Anne and Amanda
Friday, April 20th
at the Hyde Park Hotel, Knightsbridge

RSVP
The Grange,   Dancing 10.15
Little Upton,
Sussex.

Answering Invitations

A formal invitation in the third person is answered in the third person and should repeat the occasion and the date like this:

Mr and Mrs John Smith have much pleasure in accepting Mrs Alan Brown's kind invitation to a cocktail party on Tuesday May 2nd.

Or:

Miss Mary Smith has much pleasure in accepting Mrs Alan Brown's kind invitation to the wedding of her daughter on Saturday 20th July.

This is written in the middle of the paper. If your writing paper has not got an engraved heading, the modern fashion is not to write your address or the date of your reply.

If your writing paper is a large size and your acceptance looks ridiculously lost, you can fill it up by repeating the address where the party is to be held, or the name of the church.

What should you do if you receive an invitation card on which you are addressed simply as, 'Mary Smith'? Then you write back in the same style, 'Mary Smith has much pleasure in accepting Alan Jones's kind invitation', etc.

Refusing a Formal Invitation

It is considered polite to give a reason why you can't go, keeping it brief and in the third person.

Miss Mary Smith very much regrets that she is unable to accept Mrs Alan Brown's kind invitation to the wedding of her daughter on Saturday July 20th, owing to a previous engagement.

Other stock excuses are, 'owing to illness', and 'because she will be away on holiday'.

Invitations should always be answered as soon as possible so that your hostess can estimate her numbers.

OTHER CARDS

Christmas Cards

Until recently married couples who had known each other for years would exchange Christmas cards signed 'from Mr and Mrs (John Smith)'. The modern fashion is to leave out the 'Mr' and 'Mrs' and write 'from John and Mary Smith' to all but the slightest acquaintances, even though you may not address them in speech by their christian names.

Whether your names are printed or hand-written is simply a matter of personal taste and convenience. People who have their cards printed 'from Mr and Mrs So-and-so' cross out the 'Mr' and 'Mrs' and write in their christian names by hand when sending to a friend. People sending cards to close friends, of course, sign only their christian names.

The envelope of a Christmas card is never sealed.

When the card is being sent to a married couple, both names appear on the envelope.

Choosing Your Card

The sordid truth is that many people look on Christmas cards as an opportunity to show off their own taste and to judge that of their friends. If you belong to this category the cards to beware of are those covered in tinsel and gold and those with original 'poems' inside. A simple message such as 'Best wishes for Christmas and the New Year' is far safer than any original effort. Absolutely safe good-taste-wise are reproductions of famous paintings, preferably religious, since Christmas is after all a Christian festival.

But more and more people are choosing the most attractively designed card whether it has anything to do with Christmas or not. Another growing tendency is to send cards with a photograph of your house or your children. However there are pitfalls here. The couple who used photographs of Reginald in the Eton cricket eleven and in the Guards to adorn their cards did not endear themselves to the grammar-school-educated young man to whom they sent one.

What should you do if you receive a card from a friend you have accidentally left off your list? Nobody writes a thank-you letter for a card. But you can always thank the sender over the telephone.

Postcards

There is nothing against beginning, 'Dear Jim' and ending, 'Love, Mary', but most people don't. They simply say what they have got to say and sign their name or initials. 'Looks lovely, doesn't it. But wait till you hear. John & Mary.'

The great thing to remember when writing postcards is that, unlike letters, everyone feels entitled to read them.

Correspondence Cards

More and more people are discovering how useful these are for short business notes as well as brief messages to friends. Postcard size, they have the name and address of the sender printed along the top like this: 'From Lady Brown, The Grange, Little Upton, Herts.' They can be sent as postcards at postcard rates, in which case the address is written on one side and the message on the other, simply signed 'Mary Brown' or 'M.B.' without any 'Dear Sirs' or 'Yours faithfully'. Or they can be treated like ordinary writing paper and sent in sealed envelopes.

CHAPTER 9

TABLE MANNERS

GRACIE FIELDS in her autobiography recounts how she once went to a big dinner and saw her host 'Lord Somebody', breaking up his bread and putting it in his soup. Astonished, she blurted out: 'They told me never to do that, but you're doing it.'

'He was sensible, that chap,' comments Gracie Fields. ' "Good Lord, don't mind what they say," he told me. "If you like bread in your soup, put the blasted bread in." I put the blasted bread in. It seemed easy after that. I've done it ever since.'

That's all very well if you're a famous personality or an elderly peer with a reputation for eccentricity. You can afford to be a law unto yourself. But anyone else who dunked their bread at a formal dinner would provoke, if not comment, at least the odd snobbish suspicion that they hadn't been 'properly brought up'.

It's a mistake to think that the general relaxation of conventional table manners at informal servantless dinner parties applies also to the grand formal dinner. It doesn't. On formal occasions the conventions are still widely observed.

YOUR TOOLS

One of the most intimidating aspects of one's first formal dinner party is the array of cutlery on either side of one's place. Which should one use for what? A good general rule is to work from the outside to the inside and when in doubt choose the most likely implement. Cutlery should be arranged in the order in which it is to be used, so at the usual formal dinner consisting of soup, fish, meat, sweet, you will find, on your right, moving from the outside in, soup spoon, fish knife, meat knife; on your left, fish fork, meat fork. The spoon and fork for the sweet may be inside these again or above the place. The bread knife appears in a variety of positions depending on when it's supposed to be used and what for. It may be above the place; on the inside, the outside or in between the cutlery on your right. At a formal dinner when fruit follows the sweet, the fruit knives and forks may be brought in on the dessert plates after the table has been cleared.

Suppose you do use the wrong implement and find yourself with only a fish knife with which to cut the steak? Simply ask the waiter for another knife.

You may find you have been given a knife or spoon you don't need to use; with soft foods such as omelettes, rissoles or cake it is smarter to use just a fork. But, though some sweets like ice cream are eaten with a small spoon only, if dessert spoon and fork are provided, you're not supposed to use the spoon on its own. Similarly, the American etiquette of cutting up food with a knife and fork first, then leaving the knife on the edge of the plate and carrying on with just the fork is not accepted table manners over here.

When knife and fork are used together, the fork's prongs should always point down, a convention which leaves one when eating peas with a choice between spearing or mashing them on the back with the knife.

After eating, cutlery should be left tidily in the middle of the plate, spoon and fork pointing upwards, knife blade pointing inwards. Tea and coffee spoons should always be replaced on the saucer after stirring.

A very common fault is to hold a knife like a pencil. It should be held under the palm of the hand, the index finger pointing along the blade.

Finger Bowls

Useful as they are after asparagus, fruit or anything else that involves getting your fingers sticky, finger bowls are rarely used today. If you do meet one, dip only the tips of your fingers in, and dry them on your napkin.

PROBLEM DISHES

The conventional way to eat certain foods is not always the way you would expect. Here is a list of them:

Asparagus (served with melted butter). Eat it with your fingers, holding each stalk by its hard white end. Dip the green end in the butter then bite off as much as is tender. Pile the remains on the side of the plate.

Avocado Pear (served with oil and vinegar sauce). Put the sauce in the hollow of the pear, hold the shell with your fingers and spoon out the green flesh.

Birds. Bones are only picked up in the fingers on very informal occasions.

Caviare (served with toast, butter and lemon). Butter your toast, squeeze the lemon on to the caviare, pile it mouthful by mouthful on to the toast. *Caviare* (served with an omelette). A very thin omelette is put on your plate. The waiter hands round the caviare in a hollowed out block of ice. Put the caviare on the omelette, fold the omelette over. Eat it with a fork.

Cheese. Butter the bread or biscuit, pile or balance the cheese on, a bit at a time.

Corn on the Cob. This is seldom served at formal dinners as there is no un-messy way to eat it. Grasp the cob either end with your fingers—smart restaurants put a skewer in to make it easier to hold—roll it in the butter and bite off the yellow corn.

Fresh Fruit. At a formal meal, pears, apples, peaches and even bananas are pealed first then eaten with a fruit knife and fork. But on an informal occasion most people eat fruit with their fingers.

Globe Artichoke (served whole with oil and vinegar sauce). You begin with your fingers, pulling the outer leaves off one by one, dipping the white ends in the sauce and eating them, piling the green remains on the side of your plate. When you get to the soft heart of the artichoke, eat it with a fork.

Jelly. Use spoon and fork or a small spoon, never just a fork.

Lobster (served in its shell). Eat the flesh with a fish knife and fork. If the lobster comes complete with its claws, a special lobster fork is usually provided. Hold the claw with your fingers and use the special fork to get the meat out.

Melon. Slices are usually served with ginger. Sprinkle the ginger on—not too much or it can make you sneeze—use a spoon and fork or fruit knife and fork to eat the melon down to the hard part. When a half or whole small melon is served, it is generally eaten with a spoon only.

Mussels (served in their shells with a thin white wine sauce). The formal way is to eat fish and sauce together with a spoon and fork, forking the fish into the spoon. The informal way is to hold the shell in your fingers, fork out the fish, pile the empty shells on a spare plate and drink the liquid left on your plate with a spoon.

Oysters (served with red pepper and lemon). Sprinkle on the red pepper, squeeze on the lemon juice—popular fallacy has it that you can see the oyster shrink in its shell—fork out the oyster and swallow it whole.

Paté (served with toast). Butter your toast, pile on the paté mouthful by mouthful.

Smoked Salmon (served with thin brown bread and butter and lemon). Squeeze the lemon on to the salmon and eat it with a fish knife and fork, accompanied by the bread and butter.

Snails. Hold the shell with the special tongs or—if no tongs are provided—with your fingers, and fork out the flesh.

Soup. Drink it from the side of the soup spoon. Tilt the plate away from you to get at the last drops.

Spaghetti. The correct but ungraceful way is to use a fork only. Mix with the sauce, coil round the fork and shovel the spaghetti in. It's a myth that the Italians manage this any more neatly than we do, they don't.

Whitebait (served with brown bread and butter and lemon). Squeeze on the lemon. Eat them head and all with a fish knife and fork, accompanied by the bread and butter.

Roll. When served with lunch or dinner, break it and butter it piece by piece.

WHERE TO PUT . . .

Salt, mustard: On the side of the plate, never straight on to the food.

Butter, jam: On the edge of the bread plate, never straight on to the bread. No one these days observes the Victorian rule that you shouldn't eat butter with jam or butter with cheese.

Salad: On a special salad plate if you have been given one, otherwise on your meat plate.

Sauce: Whether you put it over the food or on the edge of the plate doesn't matter. What is tabu at a formal meal is mashing your food up.

Eggs cooked in individual skillets: The question is, to decant or not to decant? If you're given a plate, decant on to it. If you're not, eat them out of the skillet.

Stones, fish-bones, gristle, etc: What to do when you get one of these in your mouth? It's false politeness to swallow it. Use your fingers, your spoon or your fork—it doesn't matter which—to convey it to the edge of your plate, attracting as little attention as possible.

But if you get something stuck in your teeth there is nothing you can politely do about it.

TABLE NAPKINS

As soon as you sit down you are supposed to put the napkin on your lap to make room for the food. After a dinner party or a restaurant meal you leave the napkin unfolded on the table, since it won't be used again. But if you're staying the weekend in someone else's house, fold it. Few hostesses are going to provide guests with a different table napkin at every meal.

The same goes for hotels—if you are eating regularly in the restaurant, fold your napkin.

SMOKING

At a formal dinner, cigarettes are put out before going into the dining room and no one smokes again until after the toast to the Queen.

Whether you can get away with the American habit of smoking between courses at an informal dinner party depends on your hosts. As a whole hosts who smoke themselves tend not to mind. Non-smoking hosts often mind very much, claiming that smoking interferes with the proper enjoyment of food and wine. And anyone who smokes while drinking an expen-

sive wine is likely to be served an inferior variety next time
he comes.

So the best rule is, when in doubt, don't. Even if you know
your hosts won't object, it's polite to ask before being the first
one to light up.

But in a restaurant few people would mind if you smoked
between courses, since smoking is going on at other tables
anyway.

'FOR MR MANNERS' SAKE'

Scarlett O'Hara and her sisters in *Gone With The Wind*
were made to eat a large meal before going to a party so that
they would not display anything so vulgar as an appetite. That
fashion went out with eighteen inch waists and fainting;
'leaving a little on the plate for Mr Manners' sake' is now
considered ludicrously 'genteel'.

The problem these days when your hostess has cooked the
meal is how to avoid hurting her feelings if you're either slim-
ming or not hungry. Is it better to take what she gives you and
leave some, or to ask for a small helping? If you leave some,
your hostess may think you don't like her cooking, so it's more
tactful to ask for a little in the first place.

People allergic to any particular foods do well to warn their
hostess beforehand, otherwise she may toil all day at some
oniony masterpiece only to find that onions make her guests ill.

BEING WAITED ON

When a waiter with a dish looms up on your left, that is
your cue to help yourself, trying as far as possible not to turn
your back on your neighbour or to dig him in the ribs with
your elbow—a feat which takes a good deal of practice.

How much to take? It depends on how many people have
yet to be served—at a large formal party there are usually
duplicate dishes—and how many courses are yet to come.
Usual number of courses at a formal dinner is four—but you
can tell from the cutlery on either side of your place.

If you drop a knife or fork on the floor should you leave it
for the waiter to pick up? It depends where you are, where the
knife or fork is and how many waiters there are. While it

might seem natural to pick up your knife or fork in a restaurant it wouldn't be dignified at a formal dinner when it involved grovelling under the damask tablecloth in a tight evening dress!

ELBOWS

Is it ever permissible to put your elbows on the table? It depends how you do it. Obviously it's not good manners to sprawl, but if after the meal you like to rest one elbow on the table, even on the most formal occasions, no one could possibly object. At an informal dinner most people feel entitled to rest their elbows on the table if there's a long wait between courses, and consider anyone who disapproves as distinctly stuffy and old-fashioned.

YOUR NEIGHBOURS

Though it would be ridiculous to follow rigidly the old maxim that you should talk to the man on your right during the soup, switch to the man on your left with the fish and so on, it's obviously polite at a party, where there are too many people for the conversation to be general, to divide your attention fairly between your neighbours—even though one may be much more entertaining than the other.

How to introduce yourself if you're sitting next a stranger? One way is to offer him your place card with some remark like, 'that's who I am', when he should hand you his in exchange.

Well-mannered neighbours will see that you have everything you want but if they don't the nursery rule still holds good that you should ask rather than stretch.

ACCIDENTS

The way to treat an accident is with the minimum of fuss and apology. Supposing you spill a glass of wine; at a dinner party without servants, apologize once only to your hostess and offer to get a cloth. Probably she won't let you. She'll mop it up herself, spread a table napkin over the stained part of the tablecloth and go on with the meal as though nothing had happened. If you spill something at a public dinner, unless you spill it down your neighbour's shirt front, there is no need to apologize to anyone. The waiters will clear it up.

BREAKFAST MANNERS

This is the one meal when people feel entitled to be unsociable and read their newspapers and letters. But a polite host or hostess will ask guests if they mind.

TEA PARTY MANNERS

Tea parties today are informal affairs. But there are three small points of etiquette. It is 'not done' to crook your little finger as you drink your tea—a ridiculous affectation which is fairly considered 'genteel'. There is on the other hand no sound reason for putting the tea rather than the milk in first, but the fact remains that the more 'upper class' the home, the more likely is the milk to go in last. 'Just as it comes' is another class pointer. What you are supposed to do when your hostess asks you how you like it is to tell her exactly—'weak', 'strong' or 'very little milk, please'.

DINNER IN AN EXPENSIVE RESTAURANT

Who Goes First

It sounds complicated on paper, in practice it's the natural, common-sense thing to do. Your escort goes first into the restaurant so that he can arrange with the waiter where you are to sit. At a very smart restaurant the waiter will then show you to your table, in which case your escort brings up the rear. At a not so smart restaurant where the waiter simply indicates a table, your escort leads the way. Either the waiter or your escort should pull out your chair.

But there is a regrettable tendency among young men these days to feel that if a woman can earn her own living she can also manage to pull out her own chair!

Gigantic and mostly written in French, it is enough to shake any girl's poise the first time she goes to a smart restaurant. How many courses is she supposed to order? From which of the innumerable sections? And what on earth do Diplomate à la Crème and Bombe Glacée mean? The coward's way out is to say to your escort, 'You choose for me'. But for more adventurous spirits, here is the form.

If you choose the Table d'Hôte dinner (a set meal at a set price) it is comparatively simple. All you have to do is to choose one dish from each section. But if you choose to eat A La Carte you will probably have at least ten sections to choose from.

Nobody nowadays eats more than a three course meal except at a banquet. So choose a first course from the sections at the beginning of the menu under the headings: *Hors D'Oeuvres; Potages* (soups); *Oeufs* (eggs); *Farinages, Pâtes,* or *Pasta* (spaghetti, etc); *Poissons* (fish).

Choose a main course from the sections labelled: *Poissons* (of course if you have chosen fish as a first course you won't want it also as a main course); *Entrées* (usually but not always made dishes); *Grillades* (grills); *Rotis* or *A La Broche* (roasts), *Buffet Froid* (cold dishes).

If no vegetables come with your chosen main dish, choose vegetables or salad to be found under the labels, *Légumes, Salades* and *Pommes* (potatoes).

Choose a sweet (*Desserts* or *Entremets*) or a savoury (*Canapés*) or fruit (*Fruits*) or cheese (*Fromages*).

If you don't want three courses you are under no obligation to order them. Many people nowadays go straight into the main course, ignoring the waiter's plaintive, 'Nothing to start with?'

How to Order

Usual practice is to order the first course and main course and wait until you've finished them before ordering sweet, savoury, fruit or cheese. The woman is supposed to give her order to the man who then gives it to the waiter.

The problem when you're being treated to dinner, is knowing how much your escort is prepared to spend, whether he expects you to choose the set meal or whether you can go to town with the A La Carte menu—which includes the best dishes but comes out more expensive—without bankrupting him. The best policy is to ask, 'What are you having?' then choose a meal that comes to roughly the same price.

The girl who charitably chooses the cheapest dish on the menu may find herself watching her escort eating Lobster Thermidor while she ploughs through some humble dish she could very well have knocked up for herself at home.

THE LANGUAGE PROBLEM

Few people know what all the words on a French menu mean, but since you can't very well ask the waiter to translate everything and since, if you plunge wildly, you run the risk of spending all your escort's money on salt sod, eel or even, in France, on horse meat or frog's legs, a rudimentary knowledge of restaurant French is useful.

Dictionary of Restaurant French

A la Broche	roasted
Ananas	pineapple
Artichaut	artichoke
Asperges	asparagus
Anguille	eel
Agneau	lamb
Au Naturel	plain
Au Jus	braised
Blanquette de veau	veal in a white sauce
Beignets	fritters
Bouillabaisse	fish soup
Bar	bass
Bifteck	beef steak (though in France this is often horse)
Bécasse	woodcock
Betteraves	beetroot
Braisé	braised
Beurre	butter
Consommé	clear soup
Coquilles St Jacques	scallops served in their shells
Côtelettes	chops

131

Caneton	duckling
Canard	duck
Cervelles	brains
Cabillaud	fresh cod
Chevreuil	venison
Choux	cabbage
Chouxfleurs	cauliflower
Canapés	savouries
Crevettes	shrimps
Crêpe	pancake
Cuisses	legs (usually of chicken or frog)
Champignons	mushrooms
Chateaubriand steak	thick steak
Chevreau	kid
Civet de lièvre	jugged hare
Caille	quail
Côte de veau	veal chops
Coing	quince
Choux de Bruxelles	Brussels sprouts
Choucroute	sauerkraut
Dinde	turkey
Epinards en branche ou purée	whole leaf spinach or spinach purée
Ecrevisses	crayfish
Entrecôte	sirloin steak or cut from middle of ribs
A la brochette	on a skewer
Escargots	snails
Entremets	sweet course
Farci	stuffed
Fraises	strawberries
Foie de veau	liver
Fromage	cheese
Frit(e)	fried
Fumé	smoked
Gigot d'agneau	leg of lamb
Glace	ice cream
Glacé	iced
Grillé	grilled
Grillades	grills
Grenouille	frog
Gateau	cake
Homard	lobster
Haricots verts	French beans

132

Haricots blancs	kidney beans
Harengs	herrings
Huîtres	oysters
Julienne	vegetable soup
Jambon	ham
Jardinière	with mixed vegetables
Lard	bacon or salt pork
Levraut	young hare
Lièvre	hare
Langouste	lobster
Légumes	vegetables
Minute Steak	thin steak that's supposed to take only a minute to do
Marrons	chestnuts
Macedoine de Légumes	mixture of vegetables
Moules Marinière	mussels served in their shells with white wine sauce
Maquereaù	mackerel
Merlan	whiting
Morue	salt cod
Navets	turnips
Nouilles	noodles
Oignon	onion
Oie	goose
Omelette aux fines herbes	herb omelette
Oeufs	eggs
Perdreau, perdrix	partridge
Paté de foie gras	goose liver paté
Pommes de terre	potatoes
Poché	poached
Potage	thick soup
Poulet	chicken
Poularde	chicken
Poussin	baby chicken
Pêche Melba	peaches and ice cream
Poires	pears
Pouding	pudding
Petits Pois	peas
Poireaux	leeks
Poissons	fish
Queue de Boeuf	oxtail
Quenelles	forcemeat

Rôti	roast
Ris de veau, Ris d'agneau	sweetbreads
Ratatouille	vegetable stew with aubergines, onions and tomatoes
Riz	rice
Rognons	kidneys
Salade	salad
Soupe	soup
Sanglier	boar
Saumon	salmon
Tripe	tripe
Truffes	truffles
Topinambours	Jerusalem artichokes
Truites	trout
Thon	tunny fish
Tournedos	fillet steak
Un légume au choix	choice of one vegetable
Vinaigrette	oil and vinegar sauce
Volaille	chicken
Veau	veal

Calling Waiter or Waitress

The accepted way is to catch his or her eye, or if this steadfastly remains uncaught, to call, 'Waiter' or 'Waitress'. Clapping hands, hissing or calling 'Miss' are considered bad form.

The Wine Waiter

The tradition is for the man to choose the wine—the most he is likely to ask you is whether you'd like red, white or rosé. When he has ordered the food he asks the table waiter to send the wine waiter over. If you buy a bottle—many restaurants serve wine by the glass or in carafe, which comes cheaper— the waiter will begin by pouring a little into your host's glass for him to sample. When he has said, 'That's all right'—few men have the knowledge to say anything else unless the wine is plainly corked or sour—the waiter fills up the glasses.

It is a fallacy to suppose that it shows ignorance at an

expensive restaurant to ask the wine waiter what he recommends. Even wine connoisseurs do this.

DRINKS

How to Serve Them

Sherry. Straight from the bottle—or decanter if you prefer. If a proper sherry glass is used it is filled to the top. Serve dry or medium sherry before a meal or with the soup. Serve sweet sherry with the dessert or savoury.

Whisky. Serve it neat as a short drink or with soda as a long drink.

Gin. To two-thirds gin, add one-third tonic, lime, orange or bitter lemon—or mix it according to taste. For a *Pink Gin*, put a dash of angostura bitters in the glass first, then add neat gin. For a *Gin and It* to two-thirds gin add one-third Italian vermouth.

Dry Martini. To two-thirds gin, add one-third French vermouth. For a *Very Dry Martini*, to three-quarters gin, add one-quarter French vermouth. Stir and serve very cold with a twist of lemon peel.

Vermouths. Serve them neat as an aperitif before a meal, with soda as a long drink, or as part of a cocktail.

Dubonnet. Serve it neat as an aperitif before a meal, or with soda or tonic and sliver of lemon peel or wafer of lemon as a long drink; or in a cocktail, two-thirds dubonnet to one-third gin or vodka and a slice of lemon.

Vodka. For *Vodka on the Rocks*, serve it neat over ice, accompanied by something savoury. For a *Bloody Mary*, add vodka to ice cold tomato juice, add a dash of Worcester sauce and/or lemon juice. For a *Moscow Mule*, to one part vodka, add juice of quarter of a lemon, ice and ginger beer, garnish with lemon and stir gently. Vodka can also be drunk in any recipe you would drink gin in.

Pimms. No 1 = gin base; No 2 = whisky base; No 3 = brandy base; No 4 = rum base. For a half pint: to one measure of Pimms, marked on the bottle, add fizzy lemonade, slice of lemon, cucumber rind, borage and ice.

Rum. Serve it as a long cold drink, with ginger ale, ice and a slice of lemon; as a long hot drink with lemon squash, ginger wine, weak tea and a dash of lemon juice; as a cocktail, half rum to half orange juice, well shaken up. These are some of the most popular recipes, but there are many more to be found in recipe books.

Brandy. A good brandy should be served neat, at room temperature, as a liqueur after a meal, a little in a big glass. The glass should be warmed with the hand to release the bouquet. But brandy can also be served with soda or ginger ale as a long drink.

Vintage Port. Serve it from a decanter, at room temperature, after dinner, but before coffee and cigarettes, with unsalted biscuits, non-acid fruit, etc. It should be decanted two hours before drinking. Traditionally port is the last wine served at the dinner table, drunk by the men after the women have withdrawn, and the decanter is passed round clockwise.

Lager and Bottled Ale. These should be served chilled.

Champagne. Serve it cooled but not iced. Best method is to stand the bottle in a mixture of ice and water. Never use a champagne whisk. At a meal, champagne can be served with all courses except soup.

Liqueurs. Serve them chilled, after a meal at the same time as the coffee. Purists claim you should drink the coffee first, but most people please themselves. If a proper liqueur glass is used, it is filled to the brim.

What Wine to Drink with What

Marrying wines with food is almost as tricky as marriages between people, and almost as much has been written on the subject. Even the experts disagree on exactly which wine goes best with what. But if you stick to the following basic principles nobody can accuse you of being completely ignorant. Serve the full red wines, such as burgundy, with heavier meat dishes and game; a lighter wine such as claret with lighter meats; it is a fallacy that a red wine should never be served with white meats. With fish and shell-fish serve a fine, clear, dry, flinty white wine. But a sauce can alter the picture. Fish cooked in red wine is usually accompanied by a light red wine; meat cooked in white wine served with white wine.

Serve sherry with the soup, red wine with a strong cheese, nothing with hors d'oeuvres, avocado pear or melon. Serve a sweet white wine with the sweet. Serve a dry wine before a sweet wine, a light delicate wine before a heavier wine.

How to Serve Wine

With the course for which it has been chosen. Don't fill the glasses up to the top, leave a space for the bouquet. White and rosé wines are served chilled. Red wine is served at room temperature. The cork is removed from the wine half an hour before the meal so that the wine can breathe, which is said to improve it.

Decanting

Only old wines or vintage port need be decanted, but if you have an attractive decanter there is no reason why you shouldn't use it. Nobody nowadays ever decants because they're ashamed of the cheapness of their wine. The new wine snobbery is to be proud of knowing a good cheap wine when you meet it.

Baskets

Only excuse for using a basket is if you have an old wine and are not skilled enough to decant it—decanting is an extremely skilled business. To bring a young wine in in a basket is a pointless affectation.

How to Drink Wine

With the course with which it's served. Champagne excepted, the wine served with the meat course will rarely go with the sweet. Wine should be sipped, not gulped down. Good wine will possess a bouquet which you can inhale and enjoy before drinking. A too cold red wine can be nursed in the hand, a chilled white wine should never be.

Storing Wine

If you're going to keep it for any length of time, store the bottle in a cool place, on its side so that the cork doesn't shrink.

Glasses

Which out of the many different shapes and sizes of glasses in the shops should you choose? Wine connoisseurs agree that many of them, though attractive in themselves, are not really suitable for wine drinking. In this category come coloured, cut-glass and triangular glasses, also the conventional balloon-shaped brandy glass and flat champagne goblet.

According to the wine experts the glasses that do best justice to wine, champagne and brandy included, are plain uncoloured goblets that curve in gently at the top, thus showing off the colour and preserving the bouquet.

Traditionally there are different glasses for different wines —a long-stemmed glass for hock, a smaller, narrower glass for claret than for burgundy. But most people today make do with three glasses: one tulip-shaped goblet—a 7 oz glass being the most useful—for both white and red wines, brandy, champagne and cocktails; a 2 oz tulip-shaped goblet for sherry or, half-full, for liqueurs; a tumbler for long drinks, alcoholic or soft.

What to Ask for if You're taken out for a Drink

The problem is what to ask for if you're taken out by an impecunious boy friend. The sociable thing to do if the men are drinking beer is to drink it, too, or have cider. But if you don't like either, ask for a glass of wine or a vermouth with soda—usually, though not invariably, these come cheaper than gins, whiskies, sherries, etc.

At a Formal Dinner

You are supposed to finish your before-dinner drink before going in to the dining room.

Mixing Drinks

Since it is patently bad manners to disappear under the table, you mustn't mix your drinks. That means you mustn't mix the basic ingredients. For instance, you can mix champagne, wine and brandy, but you shouldn't mix rum with brandy, brandy with whisky or either with beer.

CHAPTER 10

PARTIES

TIMES HAVE changed since Mrs Beeton's day when five courses—soup, fish, entrée, roast meat and a choice of sweets —was the accepted number at any small dinner party. Even at banquets now more than four courses is unusual, and three —something to start with, a meat or fish dish and a sweet—is the usual number at private dinner parties, including those given by people with money and servants. People without money and servants often serve fruit or cheese instead of the sweet—the old-fashioned rule that cheese shouldn't be served at dinner being observed at banquets but rarely in the home.

The hostess's main problem is how to serve a perfectly cooked meal and still have time to enjoy her guests' company. Nothing damps the party spirit more than the sight of the hostess nervously gulping down her soup so that she can rush out to the kitchen and stir the sauce. The perfect hostess is able to sit down for a drink with her guests before serving the meal, and when she's cook and table maid as well that takes a good deal of organizing.

The best plan for unpractised cooks who can't time everything to a split second is to serve dishes that don't need last minute attention and won't spoil if guests are late or spend too long over their sherry. Soup or something that doesn't need cooking such as avocado pear or melon, some kind of stew, a sweet that can be served cold or prepared the day before and heated up.

What to serve depends on your purse. But quite inexpensive foods can be given the party touch by being cooked in a novel way. And an unusual recipe has the added advantage that it can provide a talking point if conversation gets sticky.

Good idea though it may seem, however, to use a dinner party as an excuse to experiment with an exotic new recipe rather than spending four hours and half the housekeeping trying it out on the family, experienced hostesses resist the temptation. Even the best recipes have unexpected hazards. Witness the case of a young wife who thought to impress her husband's boss with a recipe for chicken with almond sauce only to find just before he was due to arrive that the recipe included the words, 'pound the nuts'. She was still pounding the nuts with an empty milk bottle an hour later.

TINNED AND PACKET FOODS

Ready-prepared tinned and packet foods are appearing even at the 'best' dinner tables. Frozen vegetables are regularly served at Buckingham Palace and people whose cooks used to boil several lobsters for several days to make *bisque Homard* now serve packet lobster soups without a blush. The criterion today is the excellence of the food rather than whether or not it was prepared on the premises. The fact that home made mayonnaise is 'smarter' than shop mayonnaise, home ground black pepper than ready ground pepper, proper coffee than instant coffee is because these generally taste better.

THE MENU

Variety is the spice of a good meal as well as of life and the golden rule when planning the menu is to avoid repetition; potted shrimps, for instance, should not be followed by salmon, a pastry main dish by a pastry sweet, meat with a cream sauce by strawberries and cream. Colours as well as flavour and texture should be varied. Meat in a white sauce looks more appetizing accompanied by peas and carrots than by white vegetables such as leeks and boiled potatoes.

THE DRINK

Most hostesses allow quarter of an hour or so for guests to relax with a drink before dinner. This may be simply a glass of dry or medium sherry—wine experts say it should be slightly chilled but most hostesses serve it as it comes out of the bottle—or a choice of sherry, whisky and gin and something, if you can afford it.

At a four course banquet you usually get two wines, one

141

with the fish, another with the meat, possibly sherry with the soup and, if you're lucky, liqueur or brandy after dinner. But at the informal dinner party at home the most most hostesses feel called on to provide is one kind of wine served with the main course. A safe estimate is one bottle between three or, if your guests are heavy drinkers, one bottle between two. But you can get by with less if you serve a very special wine or give your guests plenty to drink before dinner. Whether to provide anything to drink after dinner depends on your purse. It's not generally expected, but it may be a welcome surprise.

Here are some sample menus including suggestions for wine to serve with the main course.

DINNER MENUS

Melon with ham or with ginger
Chicken Paprikash (chicken with a paprika and
cream sauce) rice, French beans
Apricot tart
Wine: Saint-Emilion

———

Avocado pear with oil and vinegar sauce
Roast pork, ratatouille (vegetable stew with aubergines,
onions and tomatoes), roast potatoes
Fruit salad made with white wine
Wine: Alsace Riesling, Traminer or Meursault

———

Shrimp cocktail
Osso Buco (veal stewed with dry white wine), rice
Home-made ice cream with raspberry sauce accompanied by
meringues or macaroons
Wine: Puligny-Montrachet or Alsace Riesling

HOT WEATHER MENU

Iced cucumber soup
Salmon, peas, new potatoes
Strawberries (serve them stalks removed, piled in a bowl,
sprinkled with sugar) and cream
Wine: Serve any dry white wine with the fish. Or serve
champagne with both the main course and the sweet.

The most formal way to clothe a dinner table is with a white cloth, the next most formal way is with mats on a polished surface. But many people these days for informal parties at home use a coloured cloth. (For how to lay the cutlery see page 122.)

One of the old etiquette rules rarely observed today even at banquets is that butter should not be served with rolls at dinner and that the rolls should be laid on a table napkin instead of on a plate. Butter and bread plates appear on most dinner tables today.

Wine glasses are normally laid above the knives; when there are to be several wines, the largest glass is usually put on the outside, but there is no hard and fast rule. (Water and water glasses are not laid when wine is served). If port is to be drunk with the dessert, port glasses are put with the other glasses on the table.

Traditionally liqueurs and brandy are served at the same time as the coffee after the meal in the drawing room, so the glasses should not strictly speaking be laid on the table. But to most people the liqueur or brandy is the important thing, not where it's served!

Elaborate shapes in table napkins have gone out of fashion. Today they are simply folded and laid square to the edge of the table. Linen napkins are smartest but paper ones are better than nothing.

At a big dinner party it saves a lot of passing if there are several salt and pepper pots.

When fruit is eaten after the sweet, fruit knives and forks are brought in on the dessert plates if it is a formal dinner. At the informal dinner, guests are usually expected to eat the fruit with their fingers.

In any case not many housewives these days possess fruit knives and forks. The movement is towards fewer and fewer implements; bread plates or any suitable small plates stand in for the old-fashioned curved salad plates, teaspoons do for coffee, egg and grapefruit as well. The great silver chests of Victorian times with special implements for every conceivable purpose are a thing of the past. Few people have the space to store them all or the labour to clean them.

Fish Knives and Forks

The battle of the fish knives is still on. There are those who claim they are 'distinctly common' and those who claim that ordinary steel knives spoil the taste of the fish. They are not used in Buckingham Palace, but it has been argued that this is because the royal plate dates from before the time fish knives and forks were introduced. They *are* used in many 'upper class' homes; and few inheritors of a beautiful set of silver fish knives and forks are going to be put off using them because some people might not consider them strictly 'U'.

But the controversy does mean that if you have to buy your own cutlery you can economize and use ordinary meat knives and forks instead.

Cruets

For some unknown reason, these are generally considered 'non-U', separate salt, pepper and mustard pots being considered 'U'.

Table Decorations

The best kind are small enough to allow guests a clear view of each other over the top. It's disconcerting to try and talk to someone you can see only dimly the other side of the wood.

Decanting and Dishing Up

This is a question of aesthetics rather than etiquette. Food that comes in an ordinary glass bottle, jar, tin or cardboard container looks more attractive turned out on to a dish. But there is no need to decant anything that comes in an attractive container—preserved ginger, for instance, looks perfectly nice in its own stone jar.

Aluminium saucepans are out of place on the dinner table, but there are plenty of coloured casseroles in the shops today that look just as attractive in the dining room as they are serviceable in the kitchen; and when the hostess is doing all the work they save a long pause in the meal while she dishes up.

Certain foods are always served in the dishes in which they have been cooked: souffles, steak and kidney pudding (a napkin is wrapped round the basin) and pies.

SERVING WITHOUT STAFF

The women are served before the men, the most important woman, if there is one, first, the most important man, if there is one, before the other men. Apart from this the criterion is speed and simplicity rather than etiquette. The main course is normally served in the dining room, the quickest way being for the hostess to serve out the meat while the etceteras, vegetable dishes and any gravies and sauces, are put on the table for guests to help themselves. The first course and the sweet are often brought in ready served on to the plates when this won't spoil the look of a special dish, a souffle or a tart, for instance.

It is the host's job to do any carving; if it's a bird, he gives white meat to the women, dark meat to the men, if there isn't enough white to go round. But at a large party it's not a good idea to serve something that needs carving as, by the time the host has finished, the guests' food is either cold or they are ready for second helpings.

The host also pours the wine and any drinks before or after dinner.

Even at the informal dinner most people prefer to turn their backs on the dinner table and adjourn to another room or at least to comfortable chairs for coffee. Conventionally, coffee pot, sugar basin and cream jug are brought in with small after dinner coffee cups on a tray, and guests are asked whether they would like it 'black or white?'

SERVING WITH STAFF

How much the dinner party with staff differs from the dinner party without staff depends on how many and what kind of staff you have. The formal dinner party routine with trained staff is to serve straight round the table, irrespective of sex. If there are two waiters with duplicate dishes, one can begin with the woman on the host's right, then the host and so on, the other with the man on the hostess's right, then the hostess and so on. Alternatively one can begin with the woman on the host's right and serve straight down that side of the table, while the other waiter serves straight down the other side of the table, beginning with the woman on the host's left—in which case host and hostess are served last.

Food is handed and plates are taken away on the left of each guest, but wine is poured on their right.

When there are not duplicate dishes the waiter may still serve straight round the table, beginning with the woman on the host's right, host and so on—or the women may be served first as at the dinner party without staff.

If the staff is simply the daily woman who has kindly offered to come in and lend a hand, most hostesses serve out the meat themselves while the daily hands round the vegetables.

If you're serving a joint or a bird and you have help, it saves time if you have the meat carved in the kitchen and brought in on a dish already cut up.

If there is a man servant, he pours the wine, otherwise this is still the host's job.

GUESTS

Six or eight is the usual number at the dinner party without staff. Invitation cards are only sent for very large or very formal dinners, the usual procedure being to invite people— preferably equal numbers of men and women—by telephone or by a brief letter, at least a week in advance if your guests are likely to be busy. In a house, the hostess shows the women guests up to her bedroom to leave their coats and tidy up, the host shows the men to the downstairs cloakroom. In a small flat the men's coats go in the hallway, on a peg, a chair, or over the banisters, and the bathroom is usually too obvious for anyone to need to be shown where it is.

The way to get the party off to a good start is to lose no

time getting your guests sitting down with a drink in their hands. Dinner is usually served around eight o'clock.

Seating Guests

Traditionally at a rectangular table the host sits one end, the hostess the other, but many hosts and hostesses prefer to sit opposite each other in the middle of the table. The most important woman guest sits on the host's right, the next most important on his left, the most important male guest on the hostess's right, the next most important on her left; the least important guests sit farthest away from host and hostess.

Where no one is more important than anyone else, it still saves time and confusion if the hostess tells people where to sit, arranging men and women alternately and dividing husbands from wives. At large parties the easiest way is to put a card with a name on it at each place, christian names if you're on christian name terms with your guests, otherwise, 'Mr Brown' and 'Mrs Smith'.

GOING TO A DINNER PARTY

If the hostess says, 'Come at eight o'clock', the perfect guest arrives dead on time. If she comes before she may find her hostess in the bath; if she comes after she may find the dinner is spoilt. Even the sweetest natured hostess who has watched a souffle shrink from frothy perfection to a piece of dull yellow leather while she waited for a latecomer is liable to swear that she'll never ask that person to dinner again.

But if your hostess says, 'Come at half past seven for eight o'clock', that means dinner won't be served till eight, the first half hour will be taken up with drinks, so guests can be a little late.

Going in to Dinner

At grand official dinners people still go in two by two, usually host and most important lady first, hostess and most important man last. But at private dinner parties the women go into the dining room first, followed by the men.

Offering to Help

All guests at the dinner party without staff help stacking plates at table, and passing things round. Whether they should do anything further depends on their hostess. There are hostesses who expect their guests to help wash up, but there are many more who really prefer to see their guests enjoying themselves rather than labouring over the kitchen sink and putting everything away in the wrong place. The best rule is, when in doubt offer, but don't press.

Hostesses coping with the problem of guests who insist on helping in spite of all protests can always take refuge in the white lie that the char will do it in the morning.

Again there are some hostesses who appreciate help with the fetching and carrying and final touches. But they're few and far between. All too often the guest who insists on coming into the kitchen and lending a hand is just another problem. Instead of being able to concentrate on stopping the meat from burning, the sauce from curdling and taking the sprouts off at just the right moment, the hostess has to make bright conversation or think up things for the other woman to do.

Remarks on the Food

Old-fashioned etiquette says never. This still applies at the banquet level. But when a hostess has done the cooking herself and taken a lot of trouble over a special dish, it's discouraging to have it passed over in polite silence as though it were simply meat and two veg.

Withdrawing

This old-world custom is still observed in a few households, usually those where they have a butler and an ancient nanny and expect guests to dress for dinner. If your hostess rises and murmurs, 'Shall we?' while the men sit tight, that is your cue to follow her out of the room and leave the men to their port. The women follow the hostess up to her bedroom to tidy up and discuss babies, clothes and the servant problem. The men join them for coffee and liqueurs in the drawing room anything up to half an hour later.

When to Go

The formal time to leave after an eight o'clock dinner is 10.30 to 11. But there are some hosts—mostly those who don't have to get up early the next morning—who feel the party's been a failure if guests don't stay on at least until midnight.

Thank-you Letters

There is no need to write and thank for a dinner party. But you can if you like, or want to be extra polite. The letter should be written and addressed to your hostess.

HOW TO GIVE A COCKTAIL PARTY

At the best cocktail parties the room is full but not too full for both guests and drink to circulate. A small knot of people in a large empty room is not conducive to the party spirit, but neither is a crush similar to rush hour in the tube. People tend to get frozen in the same little groups all evening because it's too hard work to move.

Traditionally a cocktail party is a stand-up affair and it's a mistake to have too many chairs. When half the guests are sitting and the other half standing, a party splits into two.

The Time

Either before lunch from 12 to 1 or before dinner from 6.30 to 8. Since few people can get away from work on a weekday morning, the before-lunch cocktail party is usually confined to Saturdays and Sundays—after church on Sunday morning is fashionable in the country. The advantage of the before lunch party is that guests arrive and leave more promptly. At a lively evening cocktail party they tend to stay on until either the drink runs out or they get hungry, which is usually nearer nine than eight.

Invitations

For a small party, invitations are made by telephone. For a large party, it's quicker to send at Home cards, see page 115. How much notice to give depends on how crowded the diaries of the people you invite are likely to be. Three or four weeks is average for a large party, a fortnight for a small one. If you give a spur of the moment party the chances are that the people you want most, your dearest friends, the wittiest men and the prettiest girls, will be otherwise engaged and you will find yourself spending a lot of time and money on comparative strangers or people nobody else wants to entertain.

Giving good notice also allows you to balance your numbers. Ideally the sexes should be nearly equal, erring on the side of a few extra men. But too many men can be fatal. Either the competition becomes unsociably fierce or they give up the struggle and retire into small masculine huddles to talk about cars.

The Drink

The usual drinks are: sherry (dry or medium)—a cocktail party is sometimes called a sherry party; whisky and soda; gin and something to go with it, French vermouth, tonic, lime juice, orange squash, etc; some soft drinks in case anyone doesn't drink alcohol. There is no reason why you shouldn't have a bigger choice of drinks if you can afford it, remembering that dry drinks are more popular than sweet.

Estimating how much drink people will get through is extremely difficult—one person will hang on to the same drink all evening and another will quaff it like water. A good way to avoid either running out or getting left with a lot of unwanted bottles is to buy on a sale or return basis. Unopened bottles go back to the off-licence and your money is refunded.

The grand way to serve drinks is for waiters to bring them round on trays. The next best thing is to inveigle a friend into acting as barman. Otherwise the only solution is to have the drink and glasses all on one table and leave guests to help themselves, which usually they show no reluctance in doing. The host if he's to talk to his guests at all can't hope to do more than see that everyone gets something to drink when they arrive and to fill up the odd glass here and there.

The Food

The traditional cocktail party snacks, stuffed olives, crisps, salted nuts, etc, are enough for the before-lunch cocktail party,

150

but in the evening the food can make all the difference between a party where people get pleasantly merry and one where they get aggressively drunk. There is no need to go to the trouble of making or the expense of buying elaborate canapés. A few sandwiches, savoury biscuits spread with paté, soft cheese or caviare, if you can afford it, or sausages on sticks, are a welcome sight to guests who may have lunched off an apple and a glass of milk. For those who haven't got anyone to hand the food round, the best plan is to distribute platefuls at strategic points round the room.

The Ash Problem

A feature of every other party is the guest who remarks with a fatuous grin that it's good for the carpet. The practised hostess provides against this by dotting ashtrays all round the room. When they're all at one end, even the best intentioned guest may find herself dropping ash on the floor.

As at any other party, some cigarettes are normally on the house, decanted out of their packets into cigarette boxes or wine glasses.

Looking after Guests

It happens to most hostesses. The food's ready, the drink's ready, she's ready. It's long past time for the party to begin and still no one has turned up. Perhaps no one will turn up at all and all her preparations have been for nothing. But invariably they do turn up, usually in a rush and then there are a hundred things to do at once.

The first thing to do is to let guests know where they can put their coats—customarily there is one room with a mirror for the women, another place for the men. The next thing is to see that the new arrivals get something to drink and someone to talk to; general introductions are possible only when there are only a few people in the room.

If you find yourself enjoying your own party, it's ten to one your guests aren't. The perfect host and hostess are constantly on the go, circulating among their guests, saying a few words to each, seeing that as nearly as possible everyone gets introduced to everyone else and nobody gets stuck with one person except from choice.

But this can be carried too far. At some parties no sooner have you been introduced to a man and got past the preliminaries of asking him what he does and what was his name, you didn't quite catch it, when you're spirited off to be introduced to someone else and have to begin all over again.

GOING TO A COCKTAIL PARTY

A peculiarity of the cocktail party is that guests are not expected to arrive on the dot. The best time to get there is about quarter of an hour late. There is nothing against arriving later except that you will probably find yourself facing a room full of strangers several drinks ahead of you while you're still cold sober.

The procedure is to dump your coat first then go in and greet your hosts who will find you a drink and someone to talk to.

Circulating

The most unrewarding type of guest from the hosts' point of view is the one who sits in a corner gossiping with the same person all evening. Guests are supposed to circulate, one of the delights of a cocktail party being that you may find yourself talking to an artist one minute and someone in the soap business the next.

How to get away from the man who seems bent on talking to you and you only all evening? The accepted and perfectly polite way is to say firmly: 'Excuse me, I must go and talk to Tom.' The coward's escape is to wait until he offers to get your glass filled up, then nip off and be deep in conversation with Tom when he returns. But the buttonholer's motive may be not your superior charm but the embarrassing fact that he doesn't know another soul there, in which case it's kind to introduce him to your friend, too.

It shouldn't happen if your hosts do their job properly, but

all too often they don't and it does. The man who was introduced to you when you arrived drifts off to talk to someone
else. There you are stranded in a room full of strangers. The
best solution is to find another woman in similar straits, go
up and introduce yourself to her.

When to Leave

When the party begins to thin out, unless you're an intimate
friend. A tired hostess doesn't welcome a comparative stranger
left on her hands to the bitter end. If on the other hand you
leave early, you may start a general exodus and break up the
party.

GOING TO A RECEPTION

Usually an official occasion, this is a grand version of the
cocktail party, with someone in livery at the door to tell you
where to put your coats, waiters to bring round the drinks and
elaborate and expensive canapés. Very little introducing is
done by the hosts except between VIPs. Other people are left
to seek out old friends or to talk to the people they brought
with them. It's not usual to say goodbye to the host or hostess
unless you've been specially invited by them. For wedding
receptions, see pages 16–18.

The Receiving Line

This is a feature of receptions, banquets and large parties
where the hosts could not otherwise manage to greet all the
guests. Here is the form. Either husband or wife gives both
names to the major-domo, 'Mr and Mrs John Smith'. If there
is a daughter as well—'Mr and Mrs John Smith and Miss
Anne Smith'. In the case of a woman with an escort other than
her husband the names are given separately. She gives hers as
'Miss Anne Smith', he gives his as 'Mr George Brown'.

When the major-domo calls your name out in a stentorian
voice that is your cue to walk in, shake hands with and say
how-do-you-do to each person in the receiving line in turn,
then pass on into the room. A wife always goes in in front of
her husband.

This has the advantage that it costs very little to give, the disadvantage that guests tend to consider that as they're contributing financially to the party they're entitled to bring whom they like and behave how they like.

The Time

After dinner, about nine o'clock.

Invitations

These are by telephone or by card (see page 117). Usually both men and girls are asked unblushingly to bring a bottle. A gallant alternative, when a good proportion of the drink is to be on the house, is to ask only the men to bring a bottle and write 'Drinks' instead on invitation cards to the girls.

What to Bring

Happy medium between spirits (generous) and beer (mean) is wine. Since you probably won't see your contribution again after handing it over to your hosts on your arrival and, since far too much mixing of drinks goes on at a bottle party for anyone to appreciate the subtle qualities of a fine wine, it's not worth spending more than 10s a bottle.

What to Provide

All you need to give a bottle party is a room, a gramophone and some glasses. But if you want to give a good bottle party you need to provide considerably more. Though the honourable course for guests is to bring as much as they're likely to drink themselves, a bottle of wine each if they're staying long, a bottle between two if they're just looking in, there are always some guests who underestimate their capacity. Hosts who want to ensure against the drink running out must provide a few bottles themselves. If you can afford to serve spirits before going on to whatever your guests have brought, it gets the party off to a good start. If any of your guests are likely to bring spirits you should lay on something to go with them.

Even the nicest people can behave abominably at bottle parties. Your best friend brings a bottle of beer and absconds with the only bottle of gin. It's an enormous help if you can persuade someone to act as barman. Otherwise there is nothing for it but to let your guests help themselves and grin and bear the resulting chaos.

Food

The most successful bottle parties always provide something to mop up the drink: sandwiches; or French bread and butter, ham and cheese or a dip, laid on a side table for guests to cut and spread themselves. Coffee and sausages are the nicest way to bring the party to a close and an indication that in the hosts' view anyway it's time to call it a night. There is however always someone who won't take the hint. The practised bottle party giver firmly refuses to let him spend the night on the sofa and if necessary rings up a taxi and puts him into it.

Pretty Girls

A fault attributed by men to girls who give bottle parties is that there are never enough pretty girls. The more pretty girls, the better the party goes—from the men's point of view anyway.

THE WINE AND CHEESE PARTY

This kind of party usually begins after dinner at about nine o'clock and includes dancing to records. The wine—red goes best with strong flavoured cheeses—may be brought by the guests on the bottle party principle or provided by the hosts. The food is usually cut-it-yourself bread and butter and a variety of cheeses, the more unusual the better.

FANCY DRESS PARTY

Though groans may be the first reaction of people suddenly faced with the headache of dreaming up a costume, fancy dress does make for a relaxed and lively party—and fancy dress parties are becoming more and more popular. What to go as?

It's a great help if the hosts give some suggestion, asking guests to come in Victorian dress, as beatniks, or as London telephone exchanges, for instance. Otherwise it's not necessary to go as anything specific so long as you look bizarre.

The trouble with brilliant ideas is that so often they're unbecoming and undanceable in. One girl who dressed up as a mushroom got first prize for originality, but her friend who went in hackneyed harem costume got all the dancing partners.

GIVING A BUFFET DINNER

The ideal way to give a buffet dinner is to have occasional tables dotted around for guests to rest their plates on, in which case you can serve anything you would at an ordinary dinner party, provided you don't have to give it last minute attention and it doesn't take too long to dish out. But few people have the occasional tables or the space.

The important thing when guests are going to have to eat off their laps or standing up is to serve food that needs little or no cutting. A rice dish that can be eaten with a fork alone is more suitable than the conventional cold meat and salad. Whether to serve the food out in the kitchen or lay it on a side table for guests to help themselves depends on the number of guests. At a large party the help yourself system, with the food attractively set out on a gaily checked cloth or scrubbed wooden table, is easiest on the hostess who has no staff.

A buffet dinner is a very movable feast. It may be given instead of an ordinary dinner party, at the end of a cocktail party, in the middle of an all evening drinks party—in fact at any time and on any occasion when you want to feed a large number of people.

AFTER DINNER DRINKS PARTY

Often this is combined with a dinner party—a few people are asked to the meal, the rest to 'come in for a drink after dinner', the idea being that just as the original guests may be running out of conversation the party is given a new lease of life. The drinks may be wine, or gin and whisky and something, or brandy and liqueurs—any alcoholic drink, in fact, that isn't an aperitif.

156

Invitations are by telephone unless it's a very large party, when at Home cards may be sent.

CHILDREN'S PARTIES

Toddlers are perfectly happy with balloons, ice creams and simple games. Older children can become absorbed in treasure hunts and charades. The most difficult age group to entertain is the seven to ten-year-old. The golden rule is to have every minute organized so that the children don't get bored and start hitting each other over the head. It's essential to write out a programme and have no intervals between items, so that Father Christmas arrives before the children have quite finished tea and the record player starts up Oranges and Lemons while Father Christmas is still doling out the last presents.

Games and tea alone are not enough to keep the children interested for the two hours or so that the party lasts. Some sort of entertainment is a must if the party is not to degenerate into a chaos of little boys pulling little girls' pigtails. Hostesses who can't afford a conjuror or a children's film can always fall back on the children's hour on the television.

Presents

The loot is an important feature. There should be prizes for at least some of the games. If it's a Christmas party all the children expect presents and if they don't get them they usually ask! If it's a birthday party all the little guests are expected to come bearing gifts. But presents and prizes need not be expensive. Quantity appeals more than quality.

The Food

Savoury sandwiches, jellies and orangeade are the mainstay of children's party teas. The younger the children the plainer the food should be. Many a mother has gone to a lot of trouble making elaborate cakes only to find her guests prefer plain brown bread and butter. It's a good idea to start the party with tea and get it out of the way. If you have a large enough table it is easier to sit the children round it than to serve the food buffet fashion.

Parents and Nannies

At a VIPs' children's party where the children are brought by nannies and nurses, the nannies and nurses are also generally given tea. At a less grand party where the children are brought by their parents, the parents are rarely asked to stay, but they are usually offered a glass of sherry when they come to collect their offspring. Considerate parents don't linger over their drink, knowing that no hostess who has just coped with the ordeal of a children's party feels like giving a cocktail party on top of it.

Clothes

Fewer and fewer parents are going to a lot of expense to deck their children out in elaborate party frocks and buster suits. The modern tendency is—since they're bound to spill something on their clothes anyway—to send them along tidy but not dressed up.

Invitations

The most trouble-saving kind are those that have a tear-off section for the reply. But any of the children's party invitations in the shops will do. Snobbery about invitation cards begins later!

Thank You's

Well brought up children should say 'thank you for a lovely party' to their hostess when they leave. Children who can be persuaded to follow this up with a thank-you letter are rare, but naturally any hostess who gets one will be delighted.

STAYING THE WEEKEND

While all hostesses wouldn't go so far as to agree with Princess Marie Louise who used to say that 'guests are like herrings; after three days they stink', it is extremely uncomfortable to feel you have outstayed your welcome. 'Come and spend the weekend' means come on Saturday in time for lunch or dinner—your hostess should indicate which—and leave after tea on Sunday, unless pressed to stay to the evening meal. If you're asked for a 'long weekend' that means you're expected to spend an extra night, arriving in time for dinner on Friday. If you're coming by train it's up to the hostess to indicate which one it will be convenient for her to meet.

What to Take

A basic wardrobe for a country weekend is a full or pleated skirt, sweater, overcoat, brogues, flat-heeled indoor shoes, high heels and a dress. If you are staying in a household where people 'change' for dinner—it's a good idea to find out if they do beforehand—the dress should be cocktail party type, otherwise take an ordinary day dress. Nightdress or pyjamas should be the kind you won't be ashamed to own if someone else makes your bed. Your hostess should let you know if she's laid on any special entertainment such as a party or a visit to the races that will require extra clothes.

Guests are expected to bring their own toothpaste, but not their own soap.

When You Arrive

Your hostess should show you to your room and leave you there while you do any unpacking or tidying up. If there's a man in the house he should carry your cases up for you. When you are ready, you come down and join the rest of the gathering.

Who Goes to Bed First?

Unfortunately there is no hard and fast rule—with the result that you sometimes get the ridiculous situation where hostess and guest both sit wearily on and on after dinner, each thinking that it's polite to let the other one break up the party. The best solution seems to be for the hostess to make the move when she sees her guests looking tired.

Breakfast

If your hostess doesn't tell you what time breakfast is, you should ask, so that you'll know when to appear the next morning. Guests who turn up before breakfast may find their hostess desperately trying to get through last night's washing up and not a bit pleased to see them.

If she offers you breakfast in bed this is probably easiest for her and it's tactful to accept. In a house with servants, it may be either a man or woman servant who carries the tray into your bedroom. So for owners of diaphanous nightdresses a knock on the door is a cue to take cover.

If you breakfast with the family it's as well to remember that many people believe, like Sir Winston Churchill, who even breakfasts separately from his wife, that this is not a time for sociable chatter. If your host hides himself behind a newspaper it's kind not to disturb him.

Entertainment

If some entertainment is laid on, you're expected to fall in with it unless you are asked if you'd rather do something else.

The Perfect Guest

If there are no servants in the house, she makes her own bed and offers to help with the washing up, but doesn't press if her offer is refused. (A guest who doesn't know where anything goes can be more nuisance than she's worth.)

She cleans the bath after using it.

If she's a young girl, she doesn't pinch what is obviously the host's chair in the sitting room.

She's always on time for meals.

She folds up the Sunday papers after reading them.

To the question: Did you sleep well? she answers Yes, even though the noise of the radiator kept her awake all night.

She doesn't wander round the house prying into the rooms on her own.

She doesn't ask for things that aren't offered to her; though there are, of course, exceptions, such as a glass of water or an aspirin for a headache.

She doesn't leave muddy footmarks on a pale carpet.

She turns off any lights she's the last person to use when she goes to bed; even millionaires have been known to object strongly when a guest left a light on all night.

Telephone Calls

The perfect guest doesn't use the telephone without asking and keeps both outgoing and ingoing calls to absolute essentials. Should you offer to pay for a call? Not for a local one, but if you have to make a trunk call, then it is tactful to offer to pay even though your hostess probably won't let you. Alternatively you can find out from the operator what the call costs and leave the money by the telephone.

Leaving

Strictly speaking you need only thank your hostess and simply say goodbye to your host, though many people thank them both. The stock reply of hostesses slightly embarrassed by a guest's thanks is, 'You must come again'. This is just a meaningless murmur of words; it doesn't mean 'invite yourself again any time you like'. The best reply is to smile sweetly or murmur, 'I'd love to', and make your escape.

What to do about your bed? Leave it with the bedclothes pulled back, to air.

As soon as possible after you get home you should write and thank your hostess.

CHAPTER 11

DRESS AND APPEARANCE

OVER THE last forty years dress along with social life as a whole has grown less and less formal. The well-dressed woman of the 1920s changed three times a day, from morning dress into afternoon dress, then into a tea gown if she was spending the evening at home, or evening dress if she was going out to dinner or the theatre.

These days, when the hostess at dinner parties is more often than not also the cook; when few people change for the theatre unless they are going to a party afterwards; when London's most exclusive nightclub no longer stipulates evening dress, it's possible for the average modern woman to be smart with comparatively few clothes. But though a large income is no longer essential, a knowledge of certain do's and don'ts still is. They are the subject of this chapter. Because the basis and first rule of all good dressing remains what it has always been: to wear the right thing at the right time and place. This is far more important than a flair for fashion. When you're the only one in taffeta and roses in a room full of tweedy coats and skirts, it's small comfort to reflect that you're wearing the latest Paris line.

TOWN AND COUNTRY CLOTHES

While town clothes are dependent on fashion, country clothes, for common sense reasons, alter very little. Hems may go up or down, but the basics remain the same. The country is wilder, wetter, colder and muddier than anyone who hasn't lived there ever dreams. So clothes must be tougher and plainer.

Flat, puddle-proof shoes, strong stockings and a skirt that can, if necessary, climb a five-bar gate, or stout slacks, are musts for a weekend or walk in the country, gumboots and a genuinely waterproof coat for a longer stay. It's smarter to be comfortable than glamorous in the country. The dowdiest person at the local gymkhana often turns out to be Lady Something-or-other!

Smart country colours, brown and tweedy mixtures, are now considered just as smart for daytime town wear as black or navy; but black and navy, for the obvious reason that they show every mark, are rarely worn out of doors in the country. Hardy annuals for country wear are camel hair coats, suede or leather jackets, tweeds, twinsets and hogskin gloves.

A word of warning to a town dweller invited to a small cocktail party in the country: find out what your hostess will be wearing. Small country parties tend to be less dressed-up than town ones. A plunging neckline can be an embarrassment.

MAKEUP

In the country this should be lighter than in town. Heavy eye-shadow, thick mascara and scarlet, pointed nails look out of place among the cows and the thistles. In town, exotic tricks—exaggerated pencilling, gold and glitter in eye-shadow and nail varnish—are best kept for evening parties.

HATS

Once you weren't considered properly dressed in town without a hat. Now most younger women consider a smart hairstyle is a better investment for everyday wear. But etiquette still demands a hat at any formal daytime occasion, in church, at weddings and wedding receptions, at garden parties at Buckingham Palace, at smart race meetings and Henley Regatta if you're sitting in the best seats, at the Fourth of June at Eton and the Eton and Harrow match at Lord's.

When should you not wear a hat? Never in your own home or in the office. If you were lunching informally in the home of friends, you would shed your hat with your coat. There are still some old ladies, however, who would consider lunch alone with them a formal occasion and expect you to arrive in a hat and keep it on.

Little hats at evening cocktail parties are optional; but if you go into the restaurant for dinner at the Dorchester or Savoy in a hat you may be asked to remove it.

GLOVES

An essential part of formal daytime wear. They are also worn on any occasion when you have to do a lot of shaking hands, if you're part of a receiving line for instance. Most people wear them to arrive at cocktail parties and balls and, except at very grand occasions, take them off afterwards if they like.

Before shaking hands, men, if they're wearing gloves, take the right one off; women keep theirs on. What to do when you're offered a drink, an olive or a cigarette? Roll the right-hand one up if it's the buttoning kind; take it off if it's not. Always take your gloves off when you sit down to dinner. Put them on again or not, as you please or as the occasion dictates, afterwards.

At one time the only gloves to wear when Royalty were present were white ones. Now they can be any colour that goes with your dress.

STOCKINGS

They should always be worn in town, even with a cotton dress. Thirty denier are smarter than fifteen denier with a ladder; it's no use wearing the ladder on the inside hoping people won't notice; they will.

SLACKS

The days when 'a trousered female' was an expression of disapproval are past. In quiet colours and patterns and on women with the right figures slacks have now become accepted and even smart for casual wear in the country and Saturday morning shopping in London. But brilliantly patterned or glittery ones should be worn only at home or at smart beach resorts.

JEWELLERY

The headmistress of an expensive French finishing school tells her pupils never to wear diamonds in the daytime. This rule, alas, affects few of us, but the principle does. The jewellery you wear should fit the clothes. Simple jewellery with casual clothes, sparkly jewellery for sparkling occasions. Necklaces and long earrings of zircons or rhinestones (closest relations in the costume jewellery world to diamonds) should be worn only in the evening, but pearls or imitation pearls are perfectly all right with jumpers and skirts.

There are fashions in jewellery as in clothes. Before the war it wasn't 'done' to wear imitation jewellery. Since the war, imitation jewellery, dignified by the name of costume jewellery, has become a fashion in its own right. Imitation is really a misnomer. Good costume jewellery is bigger and bolder than the real thing; unblushingly false, it doesn't pretend to be what it isn't.

Jewellery that's out of date can look tawdry. Long earrings in the daytime, for instance, fashionable some years ago, now look incongruous. An occasional glance at the photographs of models in the glossy fashion magazines will keep you up to date.

SCENT

A beautiful woman, a bare-shouldered evening dress, a glitter of jewellery at her ears and throat, music in the background . . . The picture would not be complete without a delicate aura of expensive scent. But, with a skirt and sweater in the office or with tweeds at an open-air sports event, the same scent can seem far too obtrusive. And even the most fabulous scent can smell horrid if worn too long—the wearer is the last person to notice it as a trip on any bus in Paris proves. The safest course is to stick to toilet water in the daytime which doesn't go stale and keep the precious little bottle of scent for evening parties.

As it's the person two paces behind, not the wearer who gets the full blast, one of the problems with scent is knowing how much to put on. Toilet water can be ladled on as lavishly as you please, but scent should be dabbed economically—on the pulse spots say the experts, where the warmth of the skin brings it out, behind the ears, on the throat, on the inside of the elbow, wrist and knees.

How should you choose your scent? Unless you are very certain of your own judgment—and even experts have said

165

that the only way to tell whether a scent is good is to live with it—it's safest to stick to the more expensive well-known brands. Or if you can't afford them, toilet water. Way to test is on the inside of your wrist, remembering that scent changes according to the skin of the wearer and a scent that may smell delightful on your best friend may not do the same for you. That is why it is wiser, too, to stick to light, flowery scents and avoid the exotic musky ones—very few women can get away with them.

A safe, if unexperimental, course is to find a scent and matching toilet water that suits you and stick to them. In time, people, especially men, come to think of it as part of your personality, rather than something that comes out of a bottle.

OFFICE CLOTHES

If it's part of a girl's job to meet people outside the firm, then her clothes are important, whether her work involves taking clients out to glamorous places for lunch or simply ushering them into her employer's room.

At the executive level the smartest wear is a tailored suit or slim dress; at a more junior level most girls find it cheaper to ring the changes with separates, straight skirts, tailored shirts and sweaters. Plain high-heeled court shoes are the smarter.

For girls who have nothing to do with people outside the firm, anything goes, but it's still smarter to look dressed for the job rather than for the beach or the evening.

CLOTHES FOR PARTIES

If the card states 'Decorations', men are expected to wear tails, and decorations if they've got any. Miniature decorations, but no neck decorations or stars, can be worn with a dinner jacket, but men who turn up like this will be in the minority.

'White tie' on an invitation card means men are expected to wear tails.

'White or black tie' means most men will wear tails but if anyone doesn't own them or feel like going to the expense of hiring them, he can get away with a dinner jacket.

166

'Evening dress' on an invitation card means that most men will turn up in dinner jackets, though you may get a sprinkling of tails, depending on the grandeur of the occasion. 'Dress optional' means that men can wear either a dinner jacket or a dark lounge suit.

Women take their cue in dressing from what the men with them are wearing. When a man wears white tie and tails, with or without decorations, women wear their grandest evening dress—long dresses are always grander than short. If a man wears a dinner jacket, a woman can wear a short or long evening dress or a cocktail dress, depending on the occasion.

When to wear your tiara if you've got one? Only when your escort is wearing white tie and tails.

When a man wears a dark lounge suit, a woman can wear a cocktail dress, but she shouldn't, strictly speaking, wear evening dress.

The golden rule, when there are no guiding words on the invitation card and you are in doubt as to what to wear, is to ask—your hostess if it's a private party, other people who are going, if it's an official occasion.

At a Dance

Official dances, dinners and evening receptions are still usually white tie occasions. But at most private dances, including all but the very grandest coming-out dances, though the older men may wear tails, the majority of the younger men wear dinner jackets.

At hunt balls of fashionable hunts non-members generally wear white tie and tails—the hunt evening dress is so glamorous that dinner jackets tend to look under-dressed—but even here some men are usually to be found wearing dinner jackets.

At dances where Scottish reels are on the programme wise women wear full skirts and medium heeled shoes. The girl who wins admiring glances in a Scottish dance is the one who never puts a foot wrong, not the girl, however gorgeous to look at, whose steps are impeded by a too tight skirt and too high heels.

Teenage Dance

To a formal dance with a band, even the youngest boys wear dinner jackets and the girls short evening dresses. But if it's an informal dancing-to-gramophone-records occasion, boys turn up in slacks and shirts or sweaters, girls in ordinary dresses or bright separates, sometimes even trousers. Wise parents check beforehand, as it takes more than the usual teenage poise to get away with a frilly party dress when all the other girls are in jeans.

Cocktail Parties

Formal wear for a cocktail party in the evening is dark lounge suits for men, cocktail dresses or suits for women—that is something more décolleté or made of a more expensive looking material than you would normally wear in the day. As more women look smarter in black than anything else this is still the most often worn colour. Practically a uniform among wives of well-to-do men is a little black dress worn with pearls and the largest piece of mink their husbands can afford.

But since so many women now have jobs which don't give them time to change, it's quite usual at a cocktail party to see a daytime suit next to an elaborate concoction in taffeta. Little cocktail party hats are worn more and more rarely today— usually only by elderly women, very chic young women who can afford the latest thing from Paris, and those who haven't had time to visit their hairdressers. Evening dress is worn at cocktail parties only by those going on to some evening dress occasion afterwards.

If the cocktail party is before lunch men still wear dark lounge suits, the most elegant women wear smart suits and frivolous hats.

Private Dinner Parties

It depends who's giving them. Generally these days if the hostess is also the cook, a man wears a dark lounge suit, a woman a nice day dress. Knocking up a last-minute sauce in a cocktail dress is liable to do neither the sauce nor the dress any good. But some people who still have servants expect their guests to turn up in dinner jackets and cocktail dresses. This sort of hostess can be very put out if you don't dress, so if in doubt, ask.

Nobody now wears a long dress to a private dinner party unless there is to be dancing afterwards.

Bottle Party

This is essentially an informal, young people's kind of party and anything goes. The average bottle party includes girls in day dresses, separates and slacks, men in sports jackets and even jeans. But where the party is by formal invitation they will be in the minority. A good deal of time, trouble and money goes into the preparation of even this humble type of party and the public-spirited thing for girls to wear is a party dress, for men a dark lounge suit. Girls with experience of bottle parties know that even the best run ones are a good deal less staid than a cocktail party and choose something gay, but not so precious and fragile that a spilled glass of red wine will be a major tragedy.

Garden Parties

Traditional garden party wear is a festive hat, silk (or its equivalent), dress, high heels and gloves. But, with the exception of those given at Buckingham Palace, formal garden parties are now rare. The modern so-called garden party is usually a means to raise money, and people wear what they please, though when a fête is dignified by this name the woman who opens it usually dresses up for the occasion.

In the Evening

At a Smart Restaurant

Men can go pretty well anywhere in London in the evening these days in a dark lounge suit. But at the very smart places for after-the-theatre-time dinner some men prefer to wear dinner jackets; at Claridges there are usually as many men in dinner jackets as in dark lounge suits. Women wear anything from a good day dress to a cocktail dress, depending on what the men with them are wearing.

At a Nightclub

At the Four Hundred, considered to be London's most exclusive nightclub, the majority of men still wear dinner jackets, but even here it's no longer obligatory. At most of the other expensive nightclubs most men wear dark lounge suits, most women cocktail dresses, though you won't get turned away if you appear in a jumper and skirt. At the comparatively inexpensive clubs that shut at midnight people turn up in whatever they please; the accent is on clothes that are casual but colourful.

At the Theatre

What you wear on an ordinary night depends on what you're doing afterwards. Practically nobody dresses just for the theatre any longer. Men and women in the front stalls who are going out to dinner or to a nightclub afterwards usually wear dark lounge suits and cocktail dresses, a very few men wear dinner jackets.

First Nights

People who have been invited, in the stalls and circle, wear dinner jackets and cocktail dresses. The general public come in ordinary clothes.

Film Premieres

Dinner jackets and cocktail dresses are usually worn in the circle, ordinary day clothes downstairs. When Royalty are going to be there, tails and full evening dress are worn by people likely to be presented to them.

Covent Garden

On gala nights, men wear white tie, tails and decorations, and women full evening dress. This applies to everywhere in the house except the gallery, which is too far away from the VIPs to be a blot on the glittering horizon. On the opening night of the season and opening nights of new productions, people wear dinner jackets and short evening dresses—there are usually a few women in long dresses as well—in all parts of the house that have access to the main foyer. In the amphitheatre and the gallery, people suit themselves—the men wearing anything from a lounge suit to a duffel coat.

On ordinary nights people wear what they would for an ordinary night at the theatre.

Glyndebourne

Men wear dinner jackets, women are supposed to wear short or long evening dresses, though not all of them do.

CLOTHES FOR SPORTS

At the Races

Anything goes if you're sitting in cheap seats or no seats at all. But if you're in the best seats, and don't happen to back a winner, a day at the races can be very expensive indeed and people come correspondingly smartly turned out, especially for the Classics. Royal Ascot and the Derby Summer Meeting excepted, women wear suits or tailored dresses and coats, small hats and high heeled shoes in summer, tweeds and furs and medium heeled shoes in winter. The smartest men wear light lounge suits in summer, tweeds in winter, and soft hats.

Royal Ascot

This is the one race meeting of the year where the fashions are more important than the horses, and no woman can be too elaborately dressed to look out of place in the Royal Enclosure. It is an occasion for silk dresses—preferably model—matching coats or mink stoles, high heels, long gloves and, of course, extravagant hats—provided the sun shines.

In theory the best dresses are supposed to be kept for Gold Cup day on the Thursday. In fact it depends on the weather. Anyone who has spent a small fortune on a model hat or dress for Ascot isn't going to miss the opportunity to wear it just because the only sunny day happens to be a Friday. And as there are always a lot of photographers around on the opening day, Tuesday, women like to wear something sensational then, too.

On uncertain days the wisest dressers wear suits and small hats, bring a more elaborate hat in the car in case. And no woman should ever go to Ascot without an umbrella. Men wear grey toppers and morning dress and look twenty times as smart as any of the women.

People in the Grandstand, Paddock and Tattersalls, which you simply pay to get into, are mostly just as smart as those in the exclusive by-invitation-only Royal Enclosure. Men can wear lounge suits in the former, but few do.

The Derby Summer Meeting

This is another grey toppers and morning dress occasion for those in the best seats. Women dress up, but not quite so elaborately as for Ascot.

Point to Points

People come prepared for the weather to do its worst, in flat shoes, tweeds, raincoats, sheepskin coats and headscarves.

Car Racing

The scene is very different from a horse race meeting. High heels and hats look out of place. The smartest thing to wear, if you're young and slim enough, is a very narrow pair of slacks and a very casual, very expensive sweater. Men wear sports jackets and slacks.

Henley Regatta

In the expensive enclosures women wear traditional garden party clothes complete with elaborate hat and high heels. Men wear rowing blazers and caps if they're entitled to them, otherwise light lounge suits. Outside the enclosures and in the boats anything goes including sun dresses and slacks. The smartest thing to wear is your prettiest cotton frock and flat heeled sandals.

The Fourth of June at Eton

Fashions are generally more tailored than for Henley. Women wear printed silk suits or beautifully cut linen 'ensembles' with small hats and high heels. A warm wrap is essential as if the weather is fine people have a picnic supper and stay on till ten o'clock watching the procession of boats and the fireworks. Men wear lounge suits, not sports clothes.

Lord's

For the university and Test matches, men wear lounge suits, most women also suits and small hats. Even at the Eton and

Harrow match, *the* social event at Lord's, this is now becoming the general rule. Fewer and fewer men each year turn up in the traditional morning dress and grey topper.

Sailing

Jeans, not too tight to move in, rubber soled canvas shoes and an oiled wool sweater, waterproof jacket or oilskin jacket and pants are the most sensible sailing wear. No pair of slacks is too old or inelegant and any old sweater will do if you're in a dinghy but, on larger boats, people tend to be smarter. At fashionable sailing clubs women change into short cotton evening dresses or gay separates for dinner and dancing in the evening. Men change into shoregoing rig, blue serge slacks or grey flannels and a reefer jacket or blazer. The owner of the boat—he is never called the skipper, as sometimes there is a paid skipper—wears black buttons, the crew brass buttons. (According to sailing etiquette the owner always buys his crew a drink when they come ashore after a race.)

Riding

It is essential when buying riding clothes for the first time to seek the advice of a firm specializing in them, since riding clothes are a law unto themselves and it is all too easy to spend money on clothes that are 'not done' in the riding world. Ginger-coloured jodhpurs, ties and tie pins with foxes heads on them for instance. Below are the correct clothes.

For Hacking. (This means simply riding as opposed to riding in the show ring or hunting field.) Tweed hacking jacket, breeches (beige) and boots (black or brown), or jodhpurs (beige) and jodhpur boots or brogues, riding bowler—not the same as a business man's bowler—shirt, plain-coloured tie, plain gold tie pin, leather or string gloves. For informal riding a roll-neck sweater can be worn with or instead of a jacket. A plain felt hat can be worn instead of a bowler or, by men, a tweed cap. Children wear a tweed hacking jacket, jodhpurs, jodhpur boots or stout shoes, shirt and tie or, informally, a roll-neck sweater, and a hunting cap (black or brown velvet).

Hunting whips are not carried unless the handle is needed

for opening gates and should never be used without the attached thong.

Hunting

People who don't hunt often enough for it to be worth while to invest in proper hunting clothes can wear tweed jacket, drab breeches, brown or black boots, stock or tie and a bowler hat. This is known by the unglamorous title of rat-catcher, and is nothing like so impervious to rain and wind as the really correct form of dress. Here it is:

For Male Members and Subscribers: Scarlet coat (no you need not call it 'pink'), white breeches, top boots, stock and top hat. Or: black coat, white breeches and top boots or drab breeches and jack boots, stock and top hat.

For Farmers: Black coat, white or drab breeches, top or jack boots, stock, hunting cap or bowler; or ratcatcher.

For Women: Sidesaddle: Blue or black habit, top hat or bowler hat, stock. Astride: Blue or black coat, drab breeches, jack boots, stock and bowler. Hunting caps are only correctly worn by Masters of Hounds—including retired masters—hunt servants and farmers, but many women wear hunting caps rather than bowlers in the belief, often mistaken, that hunting caps are more becoming. Women who are Masters of Hounds, of course, correctly wear a hunting cap whether riding side-saddle or astride.

When riding astride it is correct to wear spurs, 'dummy' with a short shank.

Children: They can wear anything they like so long as they look neat and tidy. Usually they wear tweed coat, jodhpurs, jodhpur boots, shirt, tie and hunting cap—now considered for safety's sake a 'must'.

Ski-ing

The proper ski-ing clothes, proofed trousers and an anorak jacket or one piece ski suit, are essential. Goggles need only be lightweight—some people find they don't need any a lot of the time. You also need cap or ear pads to protect your ears from the cold, oiled wool ski socks to wear inside your ski boots, ordinary woollen gloves to wear under waterproof over-

174

gloves, a warm short jacket, fur-lined boots, and thin sweaters or shirts to wear indoors.

Most women dine and dance in slacks, glamorous après ski ones in the smart resorts, worn with pretty flat-heeled evening shoes. Ordinary Saturday-morning-shopping-in-London-slacks will pass in the humbler resorts where you càn, if you like, dance in ski pants and ski boots, but it is more comfortable to have something to change into. Alternatively you can wear a gay full skirt and décolleté top.

A short dance dress may come in useful over Christmas and the New Year, otherwise it's not necessary to take a dress at all.

For people who like to be in the fashion, ski fashions change from season to season and it is as well to find out before going what's being currently worn. But it is not a good idea to wait and buy over there, since the range of clothes is bigger and the prices are generally cheaper in London.

TRAVELLING

The smart modern way to travel by train or plane is in a suit made of a crease resisting material that will emerge looking fresh at the end of the journey. For anyone flying between a cold and warm country the obvious solution is a cool dress topped by a warm coat—blankets are provided for overnight travellers, so it's not necessary to take a rug. For crossing the Channel in all but the most halcyon weather the smart thing to wear, if your figure will stand it, is slacks and a headscarf for your hair.

SMART BEACH RESORTS

On the French Riviera and in Venice, the best policy is to buy your beach clothes there, since fashions change from season to season and place to place, and English beachwear is often at least a year behind. Shorts that look quite short enough at Brighton suddenly look two inches too long when you get them down to the South of France and the three piece sunsuit that wins admiring glances at Torquay is plain dowdy at San Tropez, where no smart woman ever wears a skirt.

On the French Riviera as a whole—except at Cannes, Nice,

Monte Carlo and very expensive hotels—slacks that fit like a second skin are more often worn for dining and dancing in than skirts.

At Venice, on the other hand, it's important to have a good supply of cotton frocks, as shorts and sun tops are worn only on the Lido; they are not considered decent in the town.

The one thing it is never safe to leave behind wherever you go on the continent is a raincoat. It does rain even in places where it isn't supposed to.

SPAIN

In a country where a girl from a good family is not supposed to be left alone in a room with her fiancé, it is not surprising that there is still a great deal of prudishness about clothes. Bikinis are against the law. A girl happily sunbathing in a bikini is liable to find herself looking up at the sinister figure of an armed *guardia civil*. Shorts can be worn only on the beach—a young German caught landing on the island of Ibiza in shorts was ordered to go back and change. Slacks are all right in a small seaside resort—but any girl wearing them in an inland town may have to run the gauntlet of extremely personal remarks from Spanish men.

Spanish beach fashions are not nearly so smart as French or Italian. It is better to buy here than there.

Roman Catholic Churches

Foreigners are expected to respect the churches as churches and not treat them simply as art galleries. Anyone who goes into a church in shorts is liable to be turned out. Women are expected to cover their heads—a handkerchief will get by but obviously a headscarf is more comfortable. Bare arms are also frowned on and it's advisable to wear a cardigan.

CHAPTER 12

THE MEN IN A WOMAN'S LIFE

GOOD MANNERS FOR MEN

'A gentleman never offers a warm seat to a lady', stated a Victorian article on etiquette. Politeness is no longer carried to this fastidious extreme. But though some of the details of etiquette have changed, the basic principle remains the same: A man should always show consideration for women in every conceivable and practicable way. Here are the signs by which to recognize the perfect gentleman when you meet him.

He walks on the outside of the pavement when he's with a woman in the street. There is a common-sense reason for this —the inside of the pavement is the safest and most comfortable place, especially when cars are splashing past on a wet day.

He offers his chair to a woman when there are not enough seats to go round.

He stands up both when a woman enters and leaves a room. (Women are entitled to remain seated, but they shouldn't stick rigidly to this right; if everyone else is getting up, it looks more natural and more courteous if they get up too, particularly if the new arrivals include anyone very old or eminent.)

If a woman friend comes over to his table in a restaurant he abandons his meal and rises to his feet, unless she's considerate enough to say, 'Please don't get up.'

At the dinner table he pulls out the chair of the woman sitting next him before sitting down himself.

He offers to carry anything heavy for a woman.

He helps a woman on with her coat if he happens to be standing by when she's putting it on.

If a woman drops something he will pick it up for her.

He lights a woman's cigarette before his own. In a gathering including his wife, he lights the other women's cigarettes before hers. And if there is a box of matches handy, he lights a woman's cigarette whether he's smoking or not. Even though he's a non-smoker, he sometimes carries matches with him for this purpose.

At a party he looks after the needs of any woman he is talking to, getting her another drink, putting down her empty plate, finding an ashtray for her. If there is a buffet meal, he sees that she has something to eat before tucking in himself.

He opens a door for a woman and lets her go first except when it's more convenient for her if he leads the way. She goes first into the foyer of a cinema or theatre but he goes first into the auditorium in order to find the seats and buy the programmes. She gets into a car, a bus or a train before him, but he gets out first in order to open the door, or, if necessary, help her to alight.

But in a chauffeur driven car he gets out last, as the chauffeur will do the honours.

Naturally no man observes all the rules all the time. It just isn't practicable. Few men these days feel themselves bound to offer up their seat to a strange woman on a train or bus unless she's very old or obviously pregnant. A boss who rose to his feet every time his secretary came into the room would never get any work done. Any man who tried to follow the rules at a large party where women are constantly coming and going would be leaping to his feet all the time.

But if a man doesn't follow some of the rules some of the time, when they are practicable—particularly on formal social occasions—he's considered an oaf.

Hat Etiquette

More and more men are going without hats today. But for a man who does wear a hat there is a very definite etiquette.

He is expected to: raise it if he meets a woman he knows in the street; raise it again on taking his leave (fortunately for short-sighted women, few men today observe the old-fashioned rule that a man isn't supposed to greet a woman unless she acknowledges him first); take it off when entering a lift where there are women (many men also remove their hats when going into a women's shop); take it off when entering a

178

private house or flat and leave it in the hall or hand it to a servant if there is one.

If while driving he passes a woman he knows in a car, it would be polite to raise his hat—though, of course, safety comes first. He wouldn't risk crashing his car for the sake of etiquette!

'Sir'

In Victorian days all young gentlemen called all men senior to them 'Sir'. Today this form of address is rarely used outside the Services except by polite schoolboys, employees to their employer and young men to very much older and more eminent men who belong to a generation which still expects to be called 'Sir'.

Clothes

What a man wears has little to do with the important things like character and personal qualities, but they are an indication of what class he belongs to and the wrong clothes may place him at a social disadvantage. For anyone who wants to mix on equal terms with the English upper classes there are certain conventions of dress well worth observing.

'Loud' or 'flashy' are still socially damning epithets. The idea started in the eighteenth century by Beau Brummell that the well-dressed Englishman's clothes should be quiet and unobtrusive is still with us.

Though fashions do change even in the 'best circles'—the present trend is towards lighter suitings and a slim look, narrower lapels and ties, single breasted jackets and trousers cut to show the shape of the leg—they change so slowly and so subtly and anything new takes so long to catch on that the process is practically unnoticeable. There are many men like the Duke of Edinburgh who disdain to follow fashion at all. And a pre-war suit made by a good tailor still looks perfectly all right today.

Sad though it may be for those who long to express their personality with exaggerated lines, very tight trousers, very

179

short jackets, pointed shoes, exotically patterned ties and flashy gold watches, these are considered 'non-U'.

Hair

Oddly enough the way a man has his hair cut is also an indication of class. Though reasonably short it should never have the crude short back and sides look beloved by some barbers and, though tidy, it should never look smarmed down with hair oil. Elaborate Teddy boy styles are, of course, fashionable only in Teddy boy circles.

Brown Shoes

Only a few of the old guard cling to the view that brown shoes shouldn't be worn with anything except tweeds and country clothes. But brown shoes with a blue suit are still generally frowned on, for aesthetic reasons.

Rings and Tie Pins

At the smart London men's club level a man might wear a family signet ring, but not a ring with his initials on it. He might wear a pin with a small stud, a pearl being the most conventional, but never a clip.

Buttonholes

It's not 'done' to wear a flower with decorations. Otherwise buttonholes are simply a matter of personal taste. Before the first world war they were fashionable on most formal occasions, but now they are rarely seen except at weddings, where the bridegroom, bride's father and the ushers usually wear a white flower.

Waistcoats

The bottom button should be left undone.

Outside Breast Pocket

Pens and pencils should never be worn in the outside breast pocket. The formal thing to wear is a white handkerchief either pointed or straight; alternatively, with a tweed suit, a coloured silk handkerchief. But many younger men prefer to ignore this fashion and leave their pockets bare.

Shirtsleeves

However stifling the weather, on a formal occasion, etiquette requires a man to keep his jacket on and suffer for the sake of good manners. Even at an informal dinner party it would be polite to ask if anyone minded before he removed his jacket.

Double-breasted Jackets

All the buttons should be done up, never the inside one only.

Evening Dress

A dinner jacket (single-breasted jackets with a shawl or, more conservatively, a step collar are ousting the double-breasted type) is worn with a soft white shirt, either pleated or plain, with collar attached (it's not wrong to wear the old-fashioned stiff shirt and wing collar but it is extremely rare); a black bow tie with either pointed or, more conservatively, straight ends, usually worn outside the collar, but anyone who tucked them in would be in good company—that's how Mr Macmillan wears them; black trousers with a single row of braid; black patent leather shoes without toecaps—the Duke of Edinburgh wears black suede shoes, but this fashion has not caught on; black silk or nylon socks.

Tails are worn with a white stiff shirt with white wing collar; white bow tie; white waistcoat—waistcoat edge should never show under sides of coat; black trousers with a double row of braid; black patent leather shoes without toecaps, black silk or nylon socks. Gloves, once an essential part of evening dress are rarely, if ever, worn today.

Morning Dress

This consists of morning coat, soft white shirt with a starched linen collar, black-stripes-on-a-grey-ground trousers —alternatively, on a festive occasion, houndstooth check trousers or 'spongebags', black shoes with plain toecaps, black socks. For a funeral or memorial service, waistcoat, tie, gloves and top hat should be black. On a festive occasion, the waistcoat and gloves can be grey or buff, the tie grey silk or black with a quiet pattern; a black silk hat can be worn but a grey topper is more fashionable today.

At weddings few younger men bother with hats or gloves, especially if these have to be hired, since they will only be worn anyway for a few minutes outside the church.

MANNERS WITH THE BOY FRIEND

Who Pays?

Traditionally the man always pays for the woman. But in practice few modern young men can afford to unless their idea of entertainment is hiking through the countryside or playing football while you watch admiringly from a chilly grandstand. And this raises the problem: on what occasions should a girl offer to pay her share and when can she with a clear conscience sit back and watch him paying?

If he says: 'Will you come out with me on Saturday?' 'Will you have dinner with me tomorrow night?' or 'I've got tickets for such and such a show, would you like to come?' it's plain sailing. He's asking you out and he expects to pay for everything, including any transport, programmes if he's taking you to the theatre and any drinks in the interval. The only time you will have to put your hand in your pocket is in the ladies cloakroom.

If you meet him accidentally in a restaurant, it's plain sailing, too. He will expect you to pay for your own meal unless he's either very gallant or very rich.

But if you get an invitation of the 'Let's have lunch sometime' variety the situation is not so clear. The best policy is to offer to pay for yourself and accept gracefully if he refuses.

Going Dutch

On your first date or two with a boy friend you can reasonably expect him to treat you. But if he becomes your regular boy friend he will probably expect you to pay your share except on special celebration occasions such as your birthday, when he may say generously, 'This is on me.'

When should you hand over? Most men—even those who will ask quite blatantly for a contribution—still feel bashful about accepting money from a woman in public. The tactful time to pay up is in private, before or after the restaurant meal, not across the table, before or after the film, not in the queue.

A girl whose boy friend is among the gallant few who insist on paying every time is unwise to argue that after all she's earning just as good a salary as he is. Far better to pay him back by giving supper parties in her flat or bed-sitter, or buying theatre tickets and then asking him to come with her. Alternatively, of course, she can always knit him a sweater.

The Entertainment

If he's doing the paying, he chooses. He says, 'I thought we'd eat at such and such a place', and you're expected to trot meekly in his wake however much you loathe the restaurant of his choice. But it's just possible he may ask you where you would like to go. That may mean that money's no object with him, but far more often it means he's inexperienced in taking girls out and has not yet learned to avoid the pitfalls. If you answer honestly, you may let him in for far more than he can afford. A way out of the dilemma is either to give him a choice of restaurants at varying prices or simply to say what kind of food you fancy. 'I'd like to eat Chinese' leaves it open to him to take you to the most expensive Chinese restaurant in town or to the cheap one round the corner.

If on the other hand it's been settled that you will pay your share of the bill, you have an equal share in the choice of entertainment.

Goodnight Kisses

There you are standing on the doorstep totting up what the evening has cost him. It comes to half your week's salary. A kiss seems a small return. Girls given to this kind of reasoning should remember the moral behind the fairy story of the prince who, disguised as a swineherd, presented a musical box to the princess he was to marry. When delighted with her new toy, she thanked the supposed swineherd with a kiss, the prince refused to have anything more to do with her.

Though there are men who think in terms of a return for their money they rarely respect a girl they suspect of thinking along the same lines. Take the money spent on you as your due, thank him for a lovely evening, but don't kiss him unless you want to.

In any case though most men try, few men expect to kiss a girl the first time they take her out.

Going to a Party with a Man

If the invitation is his, then you go as his guest and you are in honour bound to let him take you home, however dull he may seem compared with the new young man you met at the party.

At the Cinema

The question, when he's treating you, is should you stand in the queue and run the risk of shaming him into buying ten shilling seats when what he had in mind was the front stalls, or should you turn your back on the queue and appear to be absorbed in the film stars' photographs? Of course it depends on the man, but if he's at all shy, the most tactful course lies with the film stars.

The Old Flame Situation

You go to a party and suddenly you see him, the old flame you lost to another girl. Filled with the bitterness of rejection, hurt pride, jealousy or embarrassment, all you long to do is turn tail and run. But the best face-saving move is to hold your ground, concentrate on making friends with the new girl in his life and when you do talk to him try to project a light-hearted well-it's-the-luck-of-the-draw attitude. More and more this is the attitude people are adopting. Men invite their old flames to their weddings these days and vice versa, and far fewer hearts are broken as a result.

Holidays

Young men and girls go on holiday alone together today without provoking any special comment. Nobody necessarily thinks the worst, and even if they do, your morals today are considered to be your own business at least as far as the world goes, though parents may have different ideas and insist on a foursome.

Man and girl usually share costs—the easiest way being to split all living expenses equally, regardless of whether her lobster costs more than his chicken or he has an aperitif and she doesn't before dinner.

But if either of them buys any clothes or presents to bring home, they pay for them out of their own money.

Putting off an Unwanted Boy Friend

If every time he rings up you say that you're busy for the next three weeks he should tumble to the fact that he's lost your interest. But if the boy friend is the type in whom hope springs eternal and you haven't the moral courage to tell him frankly you never want to go out with him again, the only way to get rid of him, and the way that will hurt his pride least, is to tell a white lie and say there is someone else.

Chasing a Man

Few people today hold the old-fashioned view that a woman who indicates a preference for a man before he's shown any special liking for her is making herself cheap. But though a girl may no longer lose the good opinion of her friends, she may lose the man if she hunts him too obviously. Most men still like to think that the initiative is theirs.

You meet a man at a party you consider may very well be the man for you. But time goes by and he doesn't ring up to ask you out. Can you ask him? No. But what you can do is invite him among a group of other people to supper, drinks or coffee. After that it's up to him.

Presents

Formerly, a nice girl would refuse any present of value from a man until she was engaged to him—any present of clothes until they were married. There is no longer any rules about what presents a nice girl should or shouldn't accept. This is one instance when the criterion really is the thought behind the gift. If a man offers you a fur coat or a flat the chances are he is not doing it purely out of the kindness of his heart. And while it may be delightful to receive a cashmere sweater from the regular boy friend it will plainly lead to

185

embarrassment if you accept one from a man you are doing your level best to drop.

MANNERS WITH YOUR HUSBAND

Though even the most model husband doesn't follow all the rules of gallantry with his wife at home—he can't be expected to jump up every time she comes into their sitting room—in public he should treat his wife just as courteously as he does other women. His behaviour should never indicate that he shares the view implied in the old music hall joke: 'Who's that lady over there?' 'That's no lady, that's my wife.'

But it's not only husbands who may be at fault. How many wives interrupt their husbands' funny stories with, 'Oh Jack you've missed the point again', or, 'That's not how it happened at all'! Husband and wife should work as a team, helping, not belittling each other and, on the surface at least, their relations should appear harmonious. The old rule about not washing dirty linen in public still holds good. However much husband and wife may long with the aid of an audience to prove once and for all how utterly unreasonable their better half is, this is embarrassing for other people.

How to refer to Your Husband

By his christian name to friends. As 'my husband' to people who don't know his christian name. You are supposed to refer to him as 'Mr Smith' or 'Sir John' only when talking to someone on a much lower social level, and even then 'my husband' is becoming more usual today. But 'Mr Smith' or 'Sir John' is the formal way to refer to someone else's husband; 'your husband' is informal.

A similar rule obtains for men when speaking of their own and other people's wives. Needless to say they should never speak of 'the wife'!

At a Party

Who decides when to go? This problem is one of the trials of the first few months of marriage. You're having the time of your life and looking forward to spending at least another hour at the party when your husband says he wants to leave. The only dignified procedure is to give in and let your husband wear the trousers in public anyway.

Making up a Foursome

The convention is for husbands and wives to split up. In the car, for instance, you sit next the other woman's husband and vice versa unless, of course, there's too little room in the back seat for this to be practicable.

CHAPTER 13

HIGH LIFE

ROYAL ETIQUETTE

Should you accidentally call the Queen Mother 'Love' or 'Dearie' when she comes to visit your council house garden, no one is going to worry—but it is more comfortable to know what you are expected to call her. Over and above ordinary good manners, there are certain conventions of behaviour observed with members of the royal family and nobody else. Of course, how far you observe these traditional formalities must depend on circumstances. If you find yourself on a ski-ing holiday or at a university dance with one of the younger members of the royal family you would not behave in the same way as you would if you were presented to the Queen or the Queen Mother on an official occasion. But it's worth noting that those most often in touch with the Queen err on the side of overdoing, rather than underdoing the formalities.

Introductions

People are always introduced to Royalty—the correct word is presented—never the other way round. The form is: 'Your Majesty (or Your Royal Highness) may I present Mr Jones', or: 'May I present Mr Jones, Ma'am (or Sir),' Ma'am is pronounced as spelt, not, as popularly supposed, 'Marm'.

Talking to Royalty

When should you address members of the royal family as 'Your Majesty' or 'Your Royal Highness' and when can you use the less formal 'Ma'am' or 'Sir'? Servants use 'Your Majesty' or 'Your Royal Highness' all the time. For everyone else the form is, in the first instance, 'Your Majesty' or 'Your Royal Highness' followed by 'Ma'am' or 'Sir'. What you should never do is to address them directly by name as 'Prince Philip' or 'Princess Margaret'.

When asking a question of a member of the royal family it is more formal to use 'Your Majesty' or 'Your Royal Highness' than 'you'. 'What does Your Majesty think of the new exhibition at the Tate?' 'Would Your Royal Highness like me to, etc.' But obviously, if you were asking a string of questions, it would sound unbearably pompous if you used 'Your Majesty' or 'Your Royal Highness' in every sentence.

Referring to Members of the Royal Family in the presence of another Member of the Royal Family

Formally, personal pronouns such as 'he', 'her', 'they', etc, are avoided, also 'husband', 'sister', 'mother', 'daughter', etc. They are referred to either by name, 'The Queen', 'Prince Philip', 'Princess Margaret', by people on a similar social level, or as 'Her Majesty', 'His Royal Highness', 'Her Royal Highness', by servants, unless, of course, there was likely to be some confusion as to who was meant.

It is a fallacy that 'you shouldn't speak to Royalty until they have spoken to you'. If you see the Queen in the street or at a party it is not good manners to go up and speak to her out of the blue. But if you are presented, there is no reason why you shouldn't speak before she does if there is an opportunity. (Usually the person doing the presenting will give the Queen a lead: '. . . Mr Smith who has been our foreman for the last twenty years', in which case it would be natural for her to speak first.) Similarly there is no reason why you shouldn't start a new topic of conversation. The Queen would probably welcome it—as usually the onus of keeping the conversation going falls on her.

Writing to Royalty

The formal way to begin a letter is: 'Your Majesty' or 'Your Royal Highness'. But people on a similar social level who have met the person they are writing to begin simply, 'Madam' to the Queen, 'Ma'am' to other female members of the royal family, 'Sir' to male members of the royal family. Among the many equally correct ways to end a letter this is a very usual form: 'I have the honour to be, Your Majesty's (or Your Royal Highness's) most humble and obedient servant.'

As in talking, personal pronouns such as 'you', or 'he' and 'her' when they refer to another member of the royal family, are generally avoided; Your Majesty, Your Royal Highness, Princess Margaret or Her Royal Highness, etc, being used instead, as in the following excerpt from a letter written by Earl Attlee to the late King:

10 Downing Street,
March 2nd, 1949

. . . Mr Churchill made the same suggestion which Your Majesty made yesterday, as to the possibility of Your Majesty being the President of India. . . .

But when this convention would result in a string of 'Your Majesties' or 'His Royal Highnesses' many people would lighten the sentence by substituting the occasional personal pronoun.

When should You Curtsey?

At the beginning and end of each meeting with the royal family. If you were presented, you would curtsey; if the Queen visited your home you would curtsey when you greeted her and when you said goodbye to her; if you had an interview with her, you would curtsey on entering and on leaving the room. If you were staying in the same house party as a member of the royal family, it would be polite to curtsey the first time you saw them in the morning and when you said goodnight. It would also be good manners to curtsey if you happened to see the Queen in a shop and she caught your eye or smiled at you. (Members of the Queen's household curtsey if they meet her in one of Buckingham Palace's passages.) At a royal garden party, when the Queen comes out of the palace, guests form a long lane. The Queen passes down it and guests bow or curtsey as she draws level with them.

How to Address the Envelope

The following styles of address have been checked with the Lord Chamberlain's Office:

Her Majesty, The Queen
Her Majesty, Queen Elizabeth, The Queen Mother

HRH The Prince of Wales
HRH The Duke of Edinburgh
HRH The Princess Royal
HRH The Princess Margaret
HRH Princess Alexandra
HRH The Princess Anne
HRH The Duchess of Kent
HRH The Duchess of Gloucester

The only royal princes entitled to 'The' after HRH are The Prince of Wales and The Prince Philip. But when a prince is also a duke (Prince Charles excepted), envelopes are addressed: HRH The Duke of ———. When a prince is not also a duke, envelopes are addressed: HRH Prince (Michael of Kent).

You should add either all honours and decorations, or none.

What to wear at a Royal Garden Party

The appropriate dress is morning coats for men, wedding type clothes for women. But there is a very strong feeling at Buckingham Palace that people shouldn't feel they have to go to a lot of expense to buy or hire special clothes in order to meet the Queen. And roughly twenty per cent of the men at a royal garden party do wear lounge suits—one of these at a garden party in 1960 was Mr Armstrong Jones. Women's clothes can be any colour they like—it is not true that they shouldn't wear black or that their gloves should always be white.

Hats and Gloves

Hats and gloves are normally worn to a daytime function when one of the royal family is present. But this is simply because these functions are formal occasions and hats and gloves are part of formal wear. When the Queen goes to horse trials or to watch polo other people come bare-headed, in headscarves or however they please. Gloves are not worn at the semi-informal dinner parties given by the Queen at Buckingham Palace.

At a Dance

When a member of the royal family is present, white tie and decorations are usually worn by the men, full evening dress and long gloves by the women; but not always.

When the dance is private or informal, the organizers get in touch with the member of the royal family concerned and ask them what they would like. They may say they would prefer people to come in dinner jackets, especially if it's a young people's dance where not many of the men are likely to possess tails.

Can a man ask a member of the royal family to dance? Not unless he's been presented to her. If he has, it is probably expressly so that he should dance with her. The polite form is: 'Ma'am, may I have the honour of this dance?'

Whether you can politely leave a party before a royal guest depends on the size of the party. At a small one it would be good manners to wait for them to leave, but if there were several hundred people no one would notice if you simply drifted off.

Dinner with a Member of the Royal Family

The royal lady, as the most important female guest, sits on the right of the host, the royal gentleman on the right of the hostess. As regards going into the dining room, it's worth noting that at semi-informal dinner parties at Buckingham Palace, the Queen and Prince Philip follow the normal procedure, the Queen going into the dining room with the women guests first, followed by Prince Philip and the men guests. But on a formal occasion where people go in two by two, the Queen goes first with her host, followed by Prince Philip and the hostess.

ETIQUETTE FOR DEBUTANTES

In spite of the social revolution that has taken place over the last decade, in spite of the fact that Buckingham Palace has set its seal on it by bringing deb's presentation parties to an end, debutantes are still with us. The ancestral home may have been turned into a lunatic asylum or a tourist curiosity, death duties and income tax may have slashed the family income so that capital will have to be sold, but Caroline still 'comes out'.

For the three months from Queen Charlotte's charity ball in May to Goodwood Races in July, which mark the end of the London Social season, she will lead a life of parties, pretty clothes and boy friends against a background of gracious living—champagne and caviare and servants to wait on her.

It is in fact a concentrated course in getting to know the 'best people'—at every party she will meet the same set and from it she will probably eventually choose her husband. Though the chances are he will be FU, old-fashioned deb slang for financially unsound—debs' mums have perforce long given up worrying about this—he will have been to the 'right' schools, have the 'right' accent and the 'right' connections.

Not that it would be fair to suggest that this is the whole purpose of giving your daughter a season. For a deb who is pretty and not too shy, the season is a fairytale interlude between school and settling down to the humdrum of everyday existence that she will never forget. It is also an opportunity to make friendships which may last a lifetime.

An increasing number of girls take the season casually, attending only a few of the star events and parties and spending the rest of the time getting on with a career. But the disadvantage of this is that a girl who doesn't go in for the full social round may find herself a wallflower at the dances she does go to.

For the deb who does the full season a job or training for a job is impossible. She may have as many as seven dances in the week ending at four o'clock in the morning, four cocktail parties, two tea parties and two lunch parties.

But invitations don't just arrive out of the blue. In order to get invited to all the smart parties, a deb has to meet more of her fellow debs than she will already know through going to an expensive school and finishing school. This usually entails a good deal of work and preliminary organization on her mother's part. Here is the pattern:

Mums' Lunch Parties

Though the eventual object of the exercise may be a husband, the Season is organized by women for women, and the whole merry-go-round is set in motion by a series of hen parties.

First, the Mums' lunches. These begin as early as November and hot up in January and February. The deb's mother invites six or eight other debs' mums whom she may have met through having had a season herself, through her daughter's finishing school, or through knowing some leading social light who knows everyone. Each of her guests will invite her back to lunch where she will meet still more debs' mums.

As with all other deb functions these lunches are on a grand scale, with drinks before lunch, wine at lunch and a hired waiter if the party takes place in a London home rather than in one of the expensive hotels or exclusive clubs.

Debs' Lunch and Tea Parties

These are the next step and their object is to bring the girls together. The deb's mother invites the daughters of the other mums she has met through the mums' lunches, so that they can meet her daughter. These parties again are mostly hen, the lunches being either sit-down or fork. Their heyday is between March and May—though lunch and tea parties given by the girls themselves for other girls go on throughout the Season.

The Dance

It is possible for a girl to have a Season if she gives only a cocktail party—especially if she's pretty and charming—but if she does give a dance, she's more likely to get asked to the other girls' dances. Most coming-out dances are held at hotels such as the Dorchester, the Savoy, Claridges and the Hyde Park Hotel, beginning between 10 and 10.30, with a sit-down supper of cold salmon, chicken in aspic and strawberries and cream at about 12.30, elaborate decorations and a band that plays on into the small hours.

The main drink is champagne but in the words of one deb: 'It's chic to serve whisky as well.' Milk, orange and lemon squashes are laid on for the debs, few of whom like alcohol. Since all this costs a minimum of three guineas a head, not counting the cost of the band, only very rich parents can afford to give a dance on their own. More often, these days, the dance is shared between two or even three girls.

Though a few coming-out dances are held before May and after September, most of them take place between these months, and the difficulty is to pick a suitable date that no one else has already booked. There is always a shortage of eligible young men, and the best dates are those when plenty of the 'right' Oxford and Cambridge undergraduates are available. Young men who have jobs can rarely afford to stay up night after night till four o'clock in the morning. Hence dances are often announced in *The Times* as early as November.

The invitations are sent out about eight weeks before the dance.

Dinner Parties

It is one of the conventions of the Season that on the night of a dance all the debs who have been invited must also be asked to dinner parties beforehand. The dance hostess has to see that they are. Usually she asks other debs' mums—a debutante's mother may have to give eight to ten dinner parties for other people's dances. But though this adds to the expense of a season, giving a dinner party is also an investment, since the girls you invite will feel in honour bound to invite your daughter to their dances or cocktail parties.

The dinner party hostess is told which girls she is to ask.

But if the dance hostess is short of young men, the dinner party hostess may have to provide her own. These new young men are then sent invitations to the dance.

For very large dinner parties, formal cards are sometimes sent, but invitations are more often by letter:

Dear Miss Montgomery-Smythe,

I am giving a dinner party at —— on ——for Lady So-and-so's dance and I should be delighted if you could come.

Miss Montgomery-Smythe writes back:

Dear Lady Blank,

I should love to come to your dinner party on Saturday, May 28th.

The dance hostess herself gives a dinner party generally in the hotel where the dance is to take place, including her daughter's closest friends and any notabilities among the guests.

But there are always some girls—ex-debs or those who have never been debs at all—who are not included in dinner parties, who simply get an invitation to the dance and that's it. When men are short these Cinderellas may also be asked to bring their own partners.

Arriving at the Dance

The dinner party, including the dinner party hostess, arrive at the same time. The men wait downstairs for the girls while they dump their wraps in the ladies' cloakroom, so that they can all go into the ballroom together. The dance hostess and her daughter will be waiting by the door to receive them.

The young men are supposed to dance with their dinner party hostess and with the girls who sat next them at dinner. A really polite young man will dance with all the girls at the dinner party; but few debs' delights carry good manners to this extreme if there are prettier girls elsewhere.

Changing Partners

As there is rarely any break in the music, this is a tricky operation. It's all done at the bar. You suggest a drink to your partner and at the bar you give him the slip for someone else. Ideally that is. But at the beginning of the season a girl who still knows very few young men may well find that it's her partner who suggests the drink and who nips off with someone else, leaving her alone with her glass of milk and her asparagus sandwich.

Her only chance of picking up another partner is to remain where she is. As one deb says: 'If you take refuge in the ladies, you're sunk. It needs a lot of courage to come back when you haven't got anyone waiting for you.

'And if you subside on to a little gilt chair on the edge of the dance floor, everyone can see that you've given up all hope. The best you can do then is to persuade one of your girl friends to keep you company.'

Leaving the Dance

Chaperoning in the full sense of the word is practically non-existent these days. The modern deb not only dances cheek to cheek without offending a single dowager, she is also generally expected to organize her own transport home. But if she can't find a man to take her, her dinner party hostess, who keeps a benevolent eye on her guests, may offer her a lift.

The dance hostess is usually much too harassed to notice the odd stranded deb.

Country Dances

Though it is often cheaper to give a dance in the country than in a London hotel, the country coming-out dance has its snags. Debs are customarily put up for the night and the dance hostess has to find neighbours willing to feed and house them. She may be lucky enough to live near other debs' mums, in which case they will probably invite the young people to stay on for the entire weekend. But debs' mums are but thinly scattered round the countryside—there are rarely enough to provide beds for some two hundred guests—and many a country vicar's wife has found herself inviting, putting up and giving a dinner party for a set of complete strangers whom she will never see again. As a last resort the dance hostess may have to hire the local inn—or she can follow the original but expensive example of the dance hostess who hired a train to bring the debs to the dance and take them back to London again in the small hours! Hiring a train for this purpose between London and Oxford for two hundred people travelling first class costs about £200!

When no provision is made for putting up guests, their mothers often club together to provide a bus or hired cars, rather than trusting to any young men their daughters may meet at the dance to bring them all the way back to London in the middle of the night.

A debutante is expected to write a thank-you letter both to her dinner party hostess and to her dance party hostess, *eg:*

Dear Lady So-and-so,
It was so kind of you to have me to dinner and such a delicious one, too. It made a wonderful start to a wonderful evening.
I hope you enjoyed the dance as much as I did.
I am so sorry not to have seen you to say goodbye.

Or:

I did so enjoy the dance. The flowers looked lovely—the colour scheme was so original—and the band was marvellous. In fact everything combined to make it a wonderful evening. I loved every moment of it.

Musts in the Season

Apart from private parties there are certain traditional events of the social Season which a deb must go to if she is not to feel out of the social swim. She must go to Queen Charlotte's ball, the white tie and tiara occasion at Grosvenor House which opens the Season. She must go to Royal Ascot for at least one day, preferably Gold Cup, and to Lord's for the Eton and Harrow match. But though most debs do go to the Fourth of June at Eton, Henley Regatta and Goodwood Races, a deb who missed these would not necessarily feel a social failure.

For a popular deb, parties don't come to an abrupt end in July. Every deb hopes to get asked to some of the Scottish dances in September. These have the advantage from the deb's point of view that dance cards are still used. Embarrassing though it may be to show a blank card when the first man asks to see it, a girl does know where she is. She can always take refuge in the ladies' cloakroom when she hasn't got a partner and emerge when she has.

After the Scottish dances, a popular deb will come back to London for the Little Season parties.

The Little Season

Wedged between the Scottish dances and Christmas there are about two coming-out dances a week in the Little Season. Some mothers prefer to give their dances then in the hope that as there aren't so many, their's will make a bigger splash.

The Deb Dress Show

One of the ways to make your mark as a debutante is to model for this annual debs' dress show organized by the NSPCC. The procedure is democratic in as far as it is possible to apply the word 'democratic' to anything as undemocratic as 'coming out'. Every deb—be her father a duke or a boiled sweets millionaire—is given a measurement chart to fill in, and the final selection is made by the dressmaker.

How to be 'Deb of the Year'

This is an artificial title created by the Press and not generally recognized by the debs themselves. While the girl may really be outstanding for her beauty, sweetness and vivacity, she may also acquire the title because her parents have deliberately sought publicity by inviting journalists to their parties. This sort of publicity seeking is considered more than a little vulgar in deb circles and, while it may influence people outside, it's not likely to win the deb friends inside.

The Deb's Wardrobe

By no means all debs' dresses are models—many of them turn up at Ascot in off-the-peg dresses. But even so a deb's wardrobe is not cheap. The evening dresses are the biggest item. The usual number is six, one grand long white one for Queen Charlotte's, another long grand one for the deb's own coming-out dance, and four not so grand, including one or two short ones. A deb also needs at least two dresses for Ascot, one grand one for Gold Cup day, another not so grand for other days. Though these Ascot dresses can be made to double for Lord's, the Fourth of June, Henley, Goodwood and cocktail parties, no deb wants to wear the same thing at every party.

Then she will have to have something to wear at deb's lunch and tea parties; she will have to have good country clothes for country weekends and point to points.

But it is possible to have too many clothes. As one deb said, explaining why the daughter of a millionaire had not been popular with the other girls, 'She was always changing her clothes'. And having a lot of girl friends is the surest way to enjoy the Season.

Deb Slang

Debs are an exclusive set and they have their own exclusive slang which changes from season to season. Among the expressions used in other years are: 'Let's hit the tiny floor'; 'cockers' for cocktails; 'news' for nice; 'a virginia creeper' for a girl who clings to her partner at a dance; 'a deadly nightshade' for a man who clings to his partner; 'old bags' for debs' mums; 'old hags' for ex-debs. There is also a fashion among debs for meaningless exaggerations. 'The dance was absolutely fabulous' and 'Jane's terribly sweet' may very well mean that the speaker was a wallflower at the dance and that Jane stole her pet young man.

INDEX

201

203

THESE ARE PAN BOOKS

K. Graham Thomson
THE PAN BOOK OF LETTER WRITING
Specially commissioned by PAN—this book is for all who wish to write fluently, concisely and with assurance. Here is the complete answer to all the problems you meet in your everyday correspondence with practical examples. A treasury of ideas and information, assembled in one handy reference book. (2/6)

G. H. Vallins
GOOD ENGLISH
This book, specially written for the PAN series, shows how to achieve a good, simple English style, whether for reports and stories or for business letters and everyday correspondence. It discusses the difficulties of the written language—punctuation, spelling, the writing of business letters, etc. (2/6)

G. H. Vallins
BETTER ENGLISH
This book enlarges on the principles of clear writing explained in the author's previous volume.
'Mr Vallins is that very rare bird—a born teacher who is not a pedant. . . . For those who want an exciting adventure among the tangled ways of usage, *Better English* could hardly be bettered'—*John o' London's Weekly*. (2/6)

Robert H. Thouless
STRAIGHT AND CROOKED THINKING
This practical book by an eminent psychologist tells you how to think clearly and avoid muddled reasoning. It exposes many dishonest tricks that are frequently used in argument, drawing the examples from controversial subjects which are often discussed today. (2/6)

PICK OF THE PAPERBACKS

THESE ARE PAN BOOKS

Dorothy Laird

HOW THE QUEEN REIGNS

In February, 1952, Queen Elizabeth II became Head of the Commonwealth. Her subjects number over 500 million. Every year she receives thirty thousand guests. She has travelled hundreds of thousands of miles throughout the world. She reads nearly as many official papers as the Prime Minister and is always extremely well-informed. Yet despite her arduous duties she derives immense pleasure from her home, her family and her friends. In this authoritative and revealing study Dorothy Laird gives a rich and inspiring account of constitutional monarchy today, and at the same time a delightful portrait of a lady of grace and vitality who is known and loved the world over. *Illustrated with 8 pages of photogravure.* (5/-)

PICK OF THE PAPERBACKS